Pool and Waterside Gardening

Pool and Waterside Gardening

A PRACTICAL GUIDE TO DESIGN, CONSTRUCTION AND PLANTING

PETER ROBINSON

Series editor John Simmons
OBE, VMH, M.Hort. (RHS), F.I.Hort., C.Biol., F.I.Biol.

CHANCELLOR
PRESS

Cover photograph: Biofotos/Heather Angel

First published in 1987. This edition published in 1994 by Chancellor Press
an imprint of Reed Consumer Books Limited
Michelin House, 81 Fulham Road, London SW3 6RB
and Auckland, Melbourne, Singapore and Toronto

ISBN 1 85152 542 4

Filmset in England by Vision Typesetting, Manchester in 11 on 12 pt Bembo

Produced by Mandarin Offset
Printed and bound in China

Contents

Preface

The Royal Botanic Gardens, Kew with their herbarium, library, laboratories and unrivalled collection of living plants, form one of the world's most important centres of botanical science. Their origins, however, can be traced back to a modest nine-acre site in the Pleasure Garden at Kew which Augusta, the Dowager Princess of Wales and mother of King George III, set aside for the cultivation of new and interesting plants.

On this site were grown many of the exotic species which reached England for the first time during this period of mercantile and colonial expansion. Trees such as our oldest specimens of *Sophora japonica* from China and *Robinia pseudoacacia* from America were planted for the Princess and still flourish at Kew, as do many accessions from Africa and Australia.

Many of Kew's earliest collectors were botanical explorers who made difficult and dangerous journeys to remote and unknown parts of the world in their search for economically important or beautiful plants. The work of Kew's botanists in gathering new species was complemented by that of Kew's gardeners, who were responsible for their care and propagation. The gardeners were also responsible for trans-shipping living plants from Kew to other parts of the world, and the Gardens rapidly became a clearing house through which 'useful' species grown in one continent were transferred to another.

At the present time, the living collections of the Royal Botanic Gardens contain approximately 50,000 types of flowering plants from every corner of the earth. Such a collection makes unending demands on the skills and dedication of those entrusted with its care. It also provides an unrivalled opportunity for gardening staff to familiarize themselves with the diverse requirements of plants from the many different climatic and geological regions of the world. The plants in the Royal Botanic Gardens are no museum collection, however. As in the eighteenth and nineteenth centuries, the Gardens continue to distribute living plant material on a worldwide basis, though they now use modern facilities such as the micropropagation unit at Kew and the Seed Bank at Wakehurst Place. The Gardens are also actively involved in the conservation of the world's plant resources and in supplying scientists at Kew and elsewhere with the plants and plant material required for their research. This may range from basic studies of the ways in which plants have evolved to the isolation of plant chemicals of potential use in agriculture and medicine. Whatever the purpose of the research, there is inevitably a need to grow plants and to grow them well, whether they be plants from the rain forests of the Amazon or from the deserts of Africa.

Your interest in gardening may be neither scientific nor economic, but I believe that the expert advice provided by specialist authors in this new series of *Kew Gardening Guides* will provide help of a quality that can be given only by gardeners with long experience of the art and science of cultivating a particular group of plants.

E. Arthur Bell
Director, Royal Botanic Gardens, Kew

Opposite: *Primula sikkimensis* by W.H. Fitch (1851) from the *Botanical Magazine* (Plate 4597)

Foreword

Gardening is in part instinctive, in part experience. Look in any village or town and you will see many gardens, balconies or even windowsills full of healthy plants brightening up the streets. However, there are always likely to be other plots that are sterile and devoid of plants, or overgrown and unloved. Admittedly gardening is laborious, but the hours spent sweating behind a mower on a hot summer's day will be amply rewarded when the smooth green lawn is admired; the painful nettle stings incurred while clearing ground will soon be forgotten when the buds of newly planted shrubs burst forth in spring.

These few examples of the joy and pain of gardening are all part of its attraction to its devotees. The successful gardeners and plant lovers of this world come to understand plants instinctively, learning their likes and dislikes, their lifespan and ultimate size, recognizing and correcting ailments before they become serious. They work with the seasons of the year, not against them; they think ahead, driven by caring, being aware of when conditions are right for planting, mowing or harvesting and, perhaps most important of all, they know when to leave well alone.

This understanding of the natural order cannot be learned overnight. It is a continuous two-way process that lasts a lifetime. In creating a garden, past masters such as Humphry Repton in the eighteenth century or Gertrude Jekyll in the nineteenth perceived and enhanced the natural advantages of a site, and Jekyll in particular was an acute observer of the countryside and its seasons. Seeing a plant in its natural situation gives knowledge of its needs in cultivation. And then, once design and planting have formed a garden, the process reverses as the garden becomes the inspiration for learning about the natural world.

With the widespread loss of the world's natural habitats now causing the daily extinction of species, botanic gardens and other specialist gardens are becoming as arks, holding irreplaceable collections. Thus gardens are increasingly cooperating to form networks which can retain as great a diversity of plants as possible. More than ever gardens can offer a refuge for our beleaguered flora and fauna and, whether a garden be great or small, formal or natural, this need should underpin its enduring qualities of peace and harmony – the challenge of the creative unison of formal and natural areas.

The authors of these volumes have all become acknowledged specialists in particular aspects of gardening and their texts draw on their experience and impart the vitality that sustains their own enthusiasm and dedication. It is hoped, therefore, that these *Kew Gardening Guides* will be the means of sharing their hard-earned knowledge and understanding with a wider audience.

Like a many faceted gemstone, horticulture has many sides, each with its own devotees, but plants are the common link, and they define this series of horticultural books and the work of Kew itself.

John Simmons
Editor

Introduction

Water, whether moving or still, can be a most challenging and satisfying medium to surround with plants and in which to grow them. A water feature offers great scope for creative design as well as providing a source of continuing interest and satisfaction; it is a form of gardening that has an enormous impact on the quality and creative use of space.

This book is intended to encourage and help those who wish to appreciate water's special contribution in gardens, from the home owner constructing or improving a water feature to readers wishing to extend their knowledge to this specialist group of plants, which bring so much freshness to gardens with their soft, lush summer growth.

The aesthetic value of water in landscape and garden design has been recognized for many years now, but more recently there has been a huge upsurge in the interest of water features for small gardens, where its additional therapeutic properties have been recognized and appreciated. The sound, movement and reflection that water provides are often enhanced by keeping ornamental fish, and the additional wildlife attracted to the garden also provides interest. As with any good composition, however, there is a fine and careful balance required to achieve harmony. Water requires this care in its planning, planting and maintenance in order to achieve conditions in which both plants and fish can flourish.

It is sometimes argued that water gardens, once established, require less maintenance for the same area than other forms of gardening. While this is largely true where maintenance is defined as physical activity, good water features will never tolerate total neglect. Even in the severe winter months, when one may be forgiven for preferring to remain indoors, leaving solid unbroken ice on the surface can be harmful, particularly to fish, and measures should be taken to ensure that a small area of unfrozen water allows the occupants to breathe. This is perhaps one reason why water has so much appeal. It also has its own character, which provides a unique opportunity to enrich our garden experience. In combining the subtle qualities of plants and water there lies a style of gardening that can stretch both the artistic and the scientific skills of the gardener to the full.

1
Water in Garden Design

Water features have long been a popular element in garden design. It would be hard to imagine many of our famous gardens without water in some form, if only as a bog garden created for contrast in a garden that would naturally be entirely dry. The water features can take many forms, depending on the size and style of the garden and the effect that is desired. If there is one part of a garden where visitors are most likely to linger, it is without doubt by the water feature. At flower shows, however, there is often a lack of sensitivity in the way water is exhibited, creating a crude dramatic effect rather than garden enhancement. Those considering the possibilities of including water in their own gardens, and looking for inspiration and ideas, are likely to be better rewarded by visiting some of the many lovely gardens open to the public.

The way water has been used successfully in other gardens can teach a good deal to those interested in incorporating a water feature – even on a very much more modest scale – in their own garden. Many examples of the contrasting use of water can be seen in gardens open to the public, where there is also plenty of opportunity to study labelled water plants that may or may not be suitable for one's own situation.

PUBLIC WATER GARDENS

When visiting gardens and noting plants it is a good idea to take note also of the plant's environment – the aspect, exposure, amount of shade, and other climatic considerations. Size and suitability can be seen at first hand, which can also be valuable. There is little point in considering growing lysichitums, for example, if one's own garden is small; seeing their fantastic size in an appropriately roomy environment will help one to avoid making such mistakes. While observing plants in other gardens, take note particularly of the depth of water in which marginal plants flourish; such information is valuable in the successful cultivation of certain species, especially primulas and irises.

The following examples of successful water features are only a fraction of the large number and wonderful variety of gardens that could be included.

Water in a formal setting
There are a number of gardens that incorporate water movement in the formal style associated with the Mediterranean, derived particularly from Spain and Italy. The gardens of Chatsworth in Derbyshire make full use of this style in the famous stepped cascade near the house. The waterfall steps, with their wide horizontal treads and shallow vertical risers, support a gentle flow of shallow water to create a leisurely and cooling effect appropriate to the Mediterranean climate and equally lovely in an English setting. A very powerful single fountain jet forms the focal point in a formal pool nearby, making water a strong element in this lovely estate.

Opposite: The splendid cascade at Chatsworth, Derbyshire, was built in 1694. Water issues from a temple at its head

One of the most impressive gardens that incorporates fountains is in the United States at Longwood Gardens, which are some 50 km (30 miles) west of Philadelphia in the historic Brandywine Valley near Kennett Square, Pennsylvania. Here, Pierre du Pont's flamboyant and extravagant use of water, influenced by his frequent trips to Italy and France, represents the ultimate expression of moving water. An unforgettable summer spectacle is provided in the night-time use of fountains, the garden terraces becoming an amphitheatre for an ever-changing, illuminated fountain display of artistic brilliance. Tropical night- and day-blooming waterlilies, including the Amazonian waterlily (*Victoria amazonica*), are also planted in a courtyard surrounded by huge conservatories, all featuring water with great effect.

Water in an informal setting

Water movement in an informal setting usually relies on watercourses and waterfalls, which are in turn often linked to large rock gardens. The Savill Garden near Windsor in Berkshire illustrates peaceful moving water in a watercourse with gentle interchanges of level and simple bridges. In spring it is the setting for the impressive architectural *Lysichitum americanum*, with its arum-like yellow flowers, and the white form *Lysichitum camtschatcense*. This early growth at the water's edge, flanked by masses of naturalized *Narcissus cyclamineus*, makes this a spring water feature well worth seeing.

Formal pools and fish

In contrast to the attraction of noise and movement, still water offers tranquillity, reflection, and the opportunity to grow waterlilies. For formal water around larger houses an opportunity is often provided by the creation of circular or rectangular pools in terraces and courtyards. Numerous gardens illustrate this feature; a good example is the Royal Horticultural Society's garden at Wisley in Surrey. In this garden a large formal water feature has been created in front of the administrative building. It is an ideal way of both reflecting the building itself and providing a home for twenty-three species and cultivars of waterlily. The tameness of the resident fish, all golden orfe, reminds one of another classic formal terrace pool – that of Bodnant Garden in Gwynedd, North Wales.

Such pools are ideal for ornamental fish, with the paving at the sides enabling the fish to be seen at close quarters. The choice of suitable fish for such pools must be made with great care. The advantage of golden orfe for these situations is their shallow swimming habit and surface feeding on insects. The carp family are less obliging. Many a water feature has been adversely affected by the introduction of koi carp, which disturb roots and shoots at the pool bottom, causing restricted plant growth and clouding of the water. Careful protection of the shoots of waterlilies and other aquatics is necessary by covering them with large cobbles. Shallow edges with thick planting should also be avoided, as expensive koi have often been stranded among foliage in the pool shallows, particularly after thunderstorms when they are often hyperactive and have a tendency to leap out of the water. if large koi are to be introduced to formal pools, consider a filter system that includes physical filtration as well as biological filtration (see page 53), and keep the sides of the pool vertical, with the water surface a few inches lower than the surrounding edge.

Waterlily gardens

For the waterlily enthusiast there are two gardens that are tremendously successful. In Humberside, in the gardens of Burnby Hall near Pocklington, are two superb lakes of waterlilies, constructed in the early 1930s. The upper pool, over half a hectare ($1\frac{1}{2}$ acres) in size, houses approximately twenty species and cultivars of waterlily, and possibly one of the best groups of the red cultivar 'James Brydon'. The lower lake, which is slightly smaller, contains just over a dozen species and cultivars, and the superb informal setting into which they blend so well makes it hard to imagine them as pools constructed of concrete.

South of the River Thames, in East Sussex, is another relatively modern garden that houses five lakes of waterlilies at different heights. This is the garden of Sheffield Park, where the waterlilies are framed by mature rhododendrons and excellent conifer groupings. This garden, like Burnby Hall, has waterlily collections maintained by experts who carefully control vigour and promote flowering by constant renewal and planting of the young crowns. In too many gardens with large lakes devoted to waterlilies the invasive varieties, particularly the native white species *Nymphaea alba*, take over the water surface, crowding out the choicer, more delicate forms and covering too much of the water surface.

Waterside planting

A garden that illustrates the lushness and diversity of waterside planting, with sensitive management to create and preserve harmony, is Wakehurst Place Garden near Ardingly in West Sussex. Wakehurst Place is a National Trust property leased by the Ministry of Agriculture, Fisheries and Food as an addition to The Royal Botanic Gardens, Kew. The geographical location, soil type and setting of this garden, backed by the expertise and resources of Kew, make this an outstanding garden to visit. Water has many moods in this setting, but it is the range of marginal and bog plants that make it a must for the plantsman. Full use is made of native plants of conservation interest, including the native tussock sedge (*Carex paniculata*), the tallest native reed-grass (*Phragmites australis*) and the equally tall and imposing water dock (*Rumex hydrolapathum*). These and many other wetland plants are carefully grouped and managed in pools and boggy areas of varying sizes and at various levels.

The origin of a cascading stream is flanked impressively by the ground cover *Polygonum affine* 'Superbum', with full use being made of this attractive genus throughout the water area to extend flowering through September. The main, almost circular pool contains an island planted with the Florida swamp cypress (*Taxodium distichum*) which is beautifully reflected in the water with the other surrounding impressive trees, shrubs and nearby mansion.

As with all good gardens, this one is full of surprises, and the picture is completed in a totally different atmosphere close to the house where a small fountain and pool form the centre point of a delightfully intimate formal garden.

Water in a romantic setting

Stourhead in Wiltshire offers a fine example of water designed into one of the first great English landscape gardens. The series of lakes, sometimes hidden, sometimes offering a breathtaking vista, were created by Henry Hoare, a London banker, in the eighteenth century. These lovely lakes in the valley are

The main fountain garden at Longwood Gardens, near Philadelphia

surrounded by mature trees and shrubs, classical temples, and grottoes. If a visit to this famous garden happens to coincide with a calm, misty morning, the visitor can experience a magic in that valley, with an atmosphere made possible only by its unique blend of romantic architecture, foliage colours and water.

Another romantic use of water has been made at Scotney Castle, near Lamberhurst in Kent (see pages 78–9). In this case a romantic fourteenth-century castle, hidden in a deep wooded valley, is surrounded by water that reflects the ruined grey castle and rust-stained tower. In this lovely estate the combination of lush landscape planting and water creates a garden of beauty and peace at all seasons.

Restoring a water feature

A smaller water garden can be found at Capel Manor in Hertfordshire. This simple pool, which was originally created by excavating gravel while Capel House was being built, provided the opportunity to blend many of water's attractions into an informal setting. Its development from an overgrown pond into today's delightful feature may have useful tips for owners of ponds in similar situations.

The water surface was almost completely covered with the native white waterlily (*Nymphaea alba*), and the water margins smothered with wild iris (*Iris pseudacorus*) fighting huge clumps of reedmace (*Typha latifolia*). In addition, on the very edge of the water was a large weeping willow (*Salix babylonica*) and numerous overgrown shrubs, including some very depressing old yews (*Taxus baccata*). In this condition the pond provided a fantastic haven for wildlife, but did very little aesthetically. Work on clearing the pond and its surroundings had to wait until mid summer to allow nests to be evacuated and the resident wild duck family to fly.

Draining began in late June, exposing a thick layer of black, silty muck forming the pool bottom. The years of decomposing vegetation from leaf fall and the rotting stems of aquatic plants had created this evil-smelling material, which was removed with the help of the local council's gully sucker, pumping and carting for nearly two days. When it had all gone the original deep pond contours were exposed, and a plan for remodelling could be drawn up. The pond had no form of lining membrane or a clay base for water retention, and was filling naturally with the water table level of the surrounding land. The weeping willow began to lose its leaves as a result of draining the pool; the decision to

The Packhorse Bridge at Wakehurst Place, Kew's 'country home' in West Sussex

remove it proved in the long term to be an extremely sensible one.

Marginal beds were created within the original deep saucer shape, and raised containers positioned in the centre to house new waterlilies. The steeper sides were contoured to provide a long-term, staged development of rock work and watercourse. The gentler sloping banking remained as lawn to allow a viewing area by the water's edge, the grass allowing the water table variation to look more natural. Development over successive years allowed creative landscaping around the sides and the introduction of more choice plants. The provision of a power supply to enable a large, surface-mounted pump to drive two watercourses, one with gentle trickling water, the other with a well-executed waterfall, allowed the pond to have movement. It now forms an element of surprise in this garden rather than a focal point, enhancing the visit.

Water features on a domestic scale

The examples of successful water features described so far can be enjoyed by the public. It is perhaps worth also describing in detail a successful water feature in a smaller private garden.

One reason why this small water garden, which is illustrated on page 43, works is its close proximity to a conservatory, housing comfortable chairs and a dining table. In all seasons, and at all times of the day, reflection, movement and noise associated with water can be enjoyed. This particular design surrounds a lean-to conservatory on the side of a bungalow and incorporates a stream, small waterfall and pool. The whole feature is enhanced by a soft red sandstone and dense planting of marginal and moisture-loving plants. It was built in two stages – the main pool construction in late summer, and the upper watercourse the following spring.

A detailed description of pool construction using a liner appears on pages 45 to 49. This procedure was followed, with two additional refinements. The first was the use of a local sandstone to edge the water line in parts of the pool on top of the liner, and the second the provision of a small foundation of setts on top of the liner but underneath the turf at the pool edge to prevent the grass and liner collapsing at this point. A further feature which makes these pools more interesting is that they are above ground level. The whole scheme is now viewed from the conservatory at eye level while sitting down. This was achieved by earth movement on a previously level site.

The upper watercourse made use of soil excavated to form a patio area around the conservatory and was contoured to create a very shallow saucer shape along the length of the watercourse. Soil placed over the edge of the liner and part way in, and mounded along the surrounding banks beyond the edge of the liner formed the planting area for both marginal and moisture-loving plants. Much of the submerged soil in the watercourse was planted with oxygenating plants, which later helped to ensure crystal clear water and to provide oxygenated water for the fish in the lower pool. Six golden orfe approximately 7.5 cm (3 in) long were introduced into the water in mid summer, rapidly consuming the rich variety of microscopic water life that had built up since the pool was made the previous autumn. They are frequently seen enjoying the slight current at the base of the waterfall, greatly enriched with oxygen from the watercourse on the upper level.

The viewpoint of the conservatory allows the dense marginal and aquatic planting to be viewed from an interesting angle, enhancing the beauty of the waterlilies.

WATER IN WILDLIFE GARDENING

As garden designers have taken account of the value of water in design, conservationists have similarly been bringing the value of water more to the fore in the encouragement and protection of wildlife in private and town gardens. It has been interesting to see the impact of exhibits at the Chelsea Flower Show and at garden festivals, where groups of volunteers have constructed and manned interesting wildlife gardens. Water used in such gardens generally needs to follow a few guidelines where priorities are given to wildlife. The slopes of the pool sides should be constructed so that there is an area of shallow 'beach' so that creatures can climb into and out of the water easily. An assortment of flat-bottomed stones should be placed near the water's edge to provide refuge for a variety of animal life. A boggy area, vital as a home to many amphibians and birds, can be created by forming a ridge in the contour of the pool liner between the deeper zone of water in the centre and a shallow area near the side, and filled with soil to accommodate plants that can then intermingle freely. Native plants should be used wherever possible, as these are known to attract wildlife more readily.

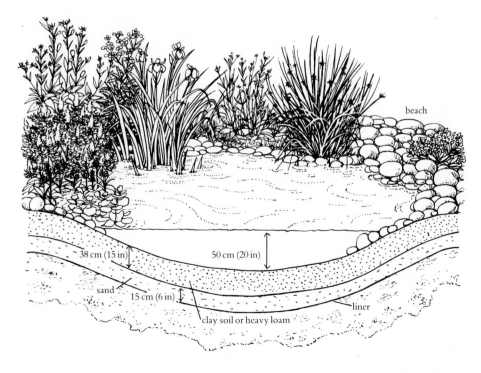

beach

38 cm (15 in)

50 cm (20 in)

sand

15 cm (6 in)

clay soil or heavy loam

liner

A wildlife pool should be surrounded by moisture-loving plants growing in soil covering the liner. The shallow edges and beach encourage birds and other creatures to come and drink and bathe. The use of indigenous plants around the margins create a welcome habitat for wildlife

2
Water Features in Gardens

Water features may take many forms depending on the style and size of garden. They may incorporate water movement, or rely upon the complete stillness so often associated with the splendour of waterlilies. They may blend naturally into an informal setting, or be modelled to fit a more structured layout. They may be the means by which the plant lover extends the range of garden plants, or be an architectural feature relying upon the strength of design or water movement alone. They may be the home for fancy fish or the outlet for budding engineers to design water courses, pump housings, filter beds and waterfalls. They may simply be a means of attracting wild life to a garden where the aesthetics are not a prime consideration. Whatever the form of water feature, there are guidelines to be observed and pitfalls to be avoided. This chapter will attempt to steer the reader in the right direction.

Movement is one of water's greatest attractions, providing not only a continuously changing appearance but also the sound of water on impact with itself or other surfaces. Until the development of increasingly efficient pumps, artificial water movement was dependent on fairly complex engineering systems in large estates where reservoirs were installed on high ground. The modern electric pump now allows water to be moved relatively cheaply, provided of course that an electric socket is reasonably close at hand. The main methods of achieving moving water are in fountains and in watercourses and waterfalls.

FOUNTAINS

Fountains tend to be more suited to formal layouts where symmetrical balance, clipped hedges and straight edges are the order of the day. Watercourses and waterfalls, on the other hand, are more appropriate to informal situations where one is attempting to copy nature.

Fountains have enjoyed an unparalleled spate of popularity in recent years, thanks partly to the mass production of extremely efficient, small, submersible pumps, which are supplied complete with a fountain rose jet and marketed in kit form. Their simplicity in installation and relatively low cost has provided a new experience for many home gardeners with the sight and sound of splashing water. There are, however, advantages and disadvantages to their use in small pools.

First, the turbulence on the pool's surface does not make ideal conditions for waterlilies and certain other aquatic plants with floating leaves. Second, the movement fountains create can be out of place if a tranquil effect is required in a semi-natural setting. They are, however, ideally suited to the circular or rectangular pool where a formal design has been achieved and the regular spray pattern produced by the fountain jet enhances the symmetrical balance. If the pool is in a hot part of the garden, the spray has a distinctly cooling effect.

Opposite: A delightful water feature framed by an archway covered with clematis and roses makes this small garden a very special place

One of the main advantages of a fountain, however, lies in its oxygenating value. A few hours of fountain operation in a small pool on a hot, sultry summer's day can have a remarkably beneficial effect on the oxygen level of the water and the consequent well-being of any fish.

When considering a standard fountain, spend time on examining the various spray patterns and effects that can be achieved. There are considerable variations possible in water droplet size, height, and spread of the spray pattern, and these factors have a large bearing on the suitability of the feature to being viewed at close quarters or from a distance. Similarly, the turbulence on the surface of the water can be kept to a minimum by using certain types of fountain jet, enabling waterlilies to be grown; the bell jet, for example, confines the spray pattern to a small area of the pool's surface, causing very little water disturbance.

Cobble fountains

A cobble fountain is a very simple and pleasant way of enjoying water movement in a small space without the need for a pool. Its effect relies upon the noise and movement of water splashing back through cobbles into a reservoir which it constantly replenishes.

The construction of a cobble fountain involves building or sinking a receptacle large enough to house a submersible pump in sufficient depth of water to cope with evaporation loss from the surface of the cobbles in hot, sunny weather. The size of the reservoir is governed by the frequency with which the system is topped up – it may even be as small as a plastic container such as the

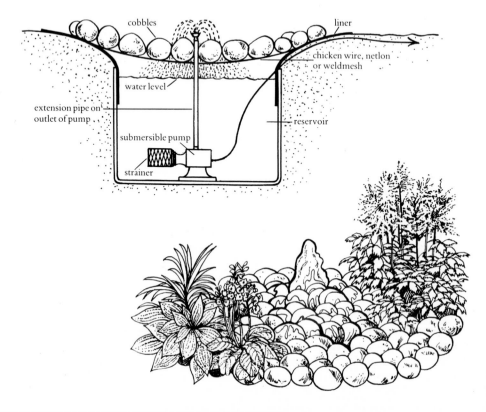

A cobble fountain is simple and inexpensive to construct. It is ideal for gardens where small children play as it is completely safe and a source of endless fascination

types used for fermenting home-made beer. After the reservoir has been sunk into the ground a waterproof membrane is positioned to surround the rim of the container in a concave shape to catch the water. The submersible pump is then inserted, with a length of hose attached to the outlet long enough to reach a few inches above ground level. A wire mesh is then placed over the top of the reservoir; it must be strong enough to bear the weight of the cobbles. The cobbles are placed at random on top of the wire mesh and the surrounding membrane. Small pieces of rock may be used as an alternative to cobbles if a 'spring' effect is required.

Millstones

As a feature for a patio, millstone fountains have a strong architectural effect and provide movement in a similar way to the cobble fountain. In this system water is pumped through the centre of the millstone and ripples over the surface of the millstone in a fine film. As the water falls from the sides of the stone it is collected in a reservoir below the millstone. Again a pool is not required; they can be built above ground level if desired, eliminating the need for any excavation. If this raised system is adopted, the reservoir tank is placed on the ground and low walls, approximately the height of the reservoir, are built around it. The cavity between the walls and the reservoir is filled with suitable material such as sand. The waterproof membrane is then placed on top of this infill material and cobble stones laid on top. Where a more turbulent or foaming effect is required, a geyser jet is used to introduce air into the water.

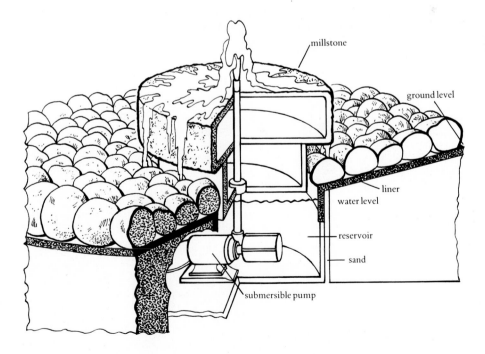

A millstone fountain is slightly more elaborate than the cobble fountain. If you are not lucky enough to find a genuine old millstone, complete kits are available that are most convincing

WATERCOURSES AND WATERFALLS

Very few garden owners are fortunate enough to have natural water running through their garden. In order to simulate this a system of pumped recirculating water may be considered. The garden's existing style, size and contours can make such watercourses fairly complex to construct, but where it is possible to incorporate them they offer enormous scope, and an opportunity to recreate that meandering, gurgling brook so much enjoyed on country walks. In addition, moisture-loving plants and rocks can be introduced alongside the water, providing one of the most interesting and creative of informal water features.

Such a feature should ideally include two basic elements: an informal approach to the remainder of the garden or surroundings, and the opportunity to create variations in level. Changes in level may already exist; if not, they can be provided by importing or moving existing garden soil.

The excavations of a large pond often provide some basic material for creating new contours, but before rushing to create the ubiquitous steep mound adjacent to the pool, a more gentle and restful treatment with a less dramatic change of height should be considered.

Opposite: This stream at Wakehurst Place illustrates the perfect use of rocks in a watercourse

Left: A small waterfall in a rock garden is not only visually attractive but sounds most refreshing on a summer's day

Designing the watercourse

As a small pool is often the natural culmination of a stream or watercourse, it also makes the starting point for designing the route. When left to its own natural devices water seldom travels in a straight line for long periods, and the design of the artificial stream will be better for taking account of this. Changes in direction can be enhanced by small waterfalls and mini pools.

Once the basic route of the watercourse has been worked out, the levels must then be carefully considered. There is little attraction in a stream where the water gushes along its length at high speed as a result of even the slightest gradient. The route should be level and meandering, allowing the water to remain in the watercourse when the circulating pump is turned off. The lowest point of each 'stream' is created by a lip or the spout of a waterfall, which allows the water to spill over when the pump is turned on but retains it when the pump is not operating.

Construction

Once the design of the watercourse/waterfall feature is beginning to take shape, there are some constructional aspects to be considered.

If the watercourse is to be constructed with a liner, and the pieces are to hand (having been measured to take into account the overlap of one piece over another at each height variation), one begins the construction at the base pool or lowest point. Flat stones can be used to create the lips for the waterfalls, and other varying pieces of rock are included to give a more natural appearance than the liner. These pieces are mortared onto the surface of the liner as the work progresses; particular care needs to be taken with the angle and overlap of the stone that forms the waterfall, as this piece makes or breaks the finished result. Patience in testing the waterflow over these points, using a hosepipe calibrated to the same approximate output as the proposed pump, will show whether the water clings to the underside of the stone as a result of too weak a flow pressure, or gushes over too quickly through too much force. Ideally one wants to achieve a gentle curtain of water which does not cause too much turbulence, and at the same time falls vertically from the stone.

The waterproofing process at the joints of the liner and rock necessitates the use of concrete or mortar and, later, sealing with a proprietary sealant paint. Where one piece of liner joins another at a waterfall it is only necessary to allow a good overlap, making sure that the lower liner is higher than the water level in the watercourse or pool.

If the surrounding soil is to be used for planting moisture-loving or bog plants by, rather than in, water, the width of the liner in the watercourses should vary to provide moist pockets. The soil is prevented from falling back into the water by pieces of rock. Such an arrangement makes the watercourses much more interesting than straight streams of even width with a grass bank at either side devoid of plants, which could luxuriate in these conditions. Vary the width of the planting at the side of the stream, as a ribbon-like band of planting can be unnatural and rather uninteresting, as can parallel rows of rocks that are obviously doing no more than disguising the edge of the liner.

As the 'ladder' of small pools is created in the watercourse, incorporate the all-important pipework to supply the circulation system. It should be included and adequately disguised at this stage, as it is much more difficult to do it afterwards. Particular attention needs to be paid to the point where the 'source' of the stream emerges. Nothing spoils the effect of a well executed and designed watercourse more than showing the supply pipe emitting water into an upper pool like a cistern. Furthermore, avoid making the upper pool at the highest point on the surrounding contours – it is far more natural to have some planting and rock effects higher than the uppermost source of the circulating water supply. The disguising of the supply pipe is a relatively easy task if some suitable rock pieces are saved to make a feature at this point.

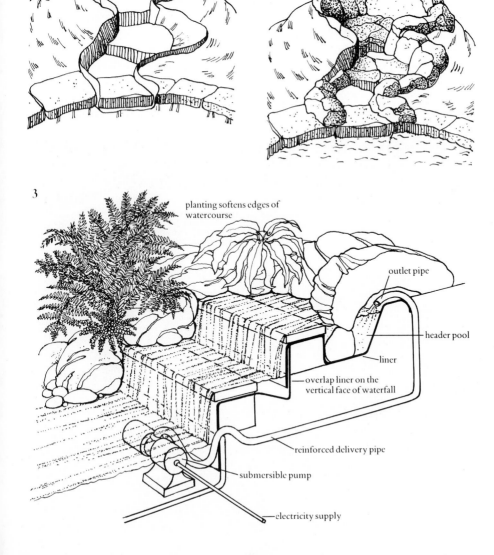

1

2

3

planting softens edges of watercourse

outlet pipe

header pool

liner

overlap liner on the vertical face of waterfall

reinforced delivery pipe

submersible pump

electricity supply

1 Prepare watercourse by shaping contours of steps into the bank and then positioning liner

2 Rocks and paving are placed in position over the liner

3 Cross-section through the finished watercourse

Pumps

When the design is complete and the watercourses have been constructed, one of the most important decisions – the choice of pump – can be made. If the curtain of water falling over the waterfalls is acceptable at 8–15 cm (3–6 in) wide and the overall height of pumped water is not above 1 m (3 ft), there is a good range of medium-priced pumps with the output to provide these requirements, i.e. an output of 12 000 litres (300 gallons) per hour. Mains water from a hosepipe can be used to assess how an output rate appears on a waterfall. The test involves pouring water from the hosepipe into a container for one minute and measuring how much is obtained. Metric rates for pump outputs are measured as litres per minute; simply multiply by sixty to convert to litres per hour. (The quantity in pints is multiplied by 7.5 to give gallonage per hour.)

Once the flow rate of the system has been ascertained and the overall head of water (the height from the pool surface to the highest point of discharge) checked, there are many types of pump to choose from. There is an important difference in performance requirements between a pump for a waterfall, where the volume of water being moved is paramount, and a fountain, where the pressure of water being forced to a given height is critical. A further consideration, particularly for watercourses where the water may have to be pumped fair distances, is the bore size of the outlet pipe from the pump to the furthest point of the system. For a flow rate of up to 440 litres (120 gal) per hour, 1 cm ($\frac{1}{2}$ in) tubing is generally adequate. For up to 1600 litres (350 gal) per hour

Opposite: Water has a place in any garden. This small enclosed patio with its raised pool and fountain provides a welcome haven from the bustle of the city

Right: A series of small waterfalls pour into a second, more informal, pool. The pebble beach and *Acer palmatum* 'Dissectum' give a Japanese feel to this modern feature

2 cm ($\frac{3}{4}$ in) bore is adequate, and for up to 4500 litres (1000 gal) per hour 2.5 cm (1 in) pipe is recommended. The bore size continues to rise in relation to flow rates, but it would be prudent to consider a slightly larger bore than may be the minimum requirement, particularly where the water has some distance to travel in addition to height.

It is also sensible not to have a pump changing the water of a base pool too frequently. To help maintain the correct balance of living organisms in the water, the flow rate per hour should not exceed the pool volume. Therefore a base pool of 12 000 litres (300 gal) capacity should preferably have a pump driving less than 12 000 (300 gal) per hour round the system. (A rough guide to ascertaining pond volume in litres/metres is to multiply the measurements in feet of length by depth by width, then further multiply by 1000. Alternatively, multiply length by depth by width in feet, and then multiply by six to obtain pond volume in gallons.)

There are two main types of pump used for water features – submersible pumps and surface mounted pumps. Submersible pumps are positioned under the water in the base pool or the lowest point of the system, preferably a few inches above the pool bottom on a small plinth to reduce the risk of leaves and other debris being sucked into the inlet strainer of the pump. They are simple to install: the outlet pipe needs to be connected to the pump, and the pump's electrical lead is taken to an adjacent waterproof connector suitably disguised under rock, paving or planting. Ensure that this is an earthed connection, preferably a proprietary weatherproof connector which leads to an earthed socket that complies with the official specifications.

Submersible pumps are prone to sucking debris into their integral strainer, which should be cleaned from time to time as the pump's performance is hindered by a dirty inlet. Advances in the design of submersible pumps has reduced this problem: the strainer now resembles a hedgehog, with several external spikes that catch the offending leaves before they can block the inlet holes. Submersible pumps should never be allowed to run dry; if they are required for continuous running of the waterfalls, ensure that they are recommended by a specialist for this type of operation. They are particularly suitable for the small pool owner who requires simple and quick installation, intermittent use, and relative ease to adapt or add for fountain use. They range from modest flow rates of about 450 litres (100 gal) per hour over a 1.5 m (5 ft) head to models that will pump over 22 500 litres (5000 gal) per hour over the same head, so there are models available that can cope with the needs of most watercourses.

Surface pumps, with their surrounding pump chambers and additional plumbing, may appear initially less attractive than the easily installed submersible pumps. Closer investigation will, however, reveal that the surface pumps have some advantages. The induction types are more suited to continuous operation over a long period, and they produce relatively higher pressure than a similar submersible pump, so could be more appropriate where a high head of circulation is required.

Surface pumps should be housed in a well constructed, waterproof chamber near to the pool, allowing for as short a length as possible of straight suction pipe. The housing chamber should be well ventilated to prevent too much

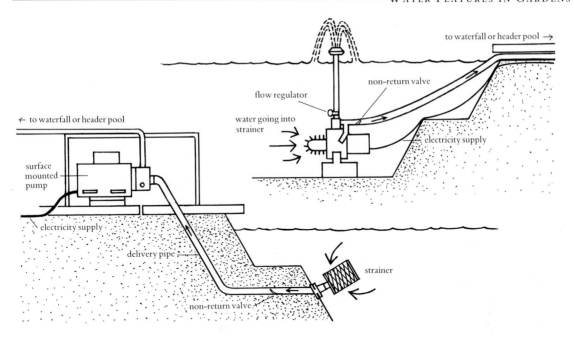

moisture and condensation building up around the pump, which frequently causes deterioration. It is a useful bonus if the housing chamber incorporates an electric socket for other accessories that may be added·later. The suction pipe to the pool or reservoir must have a strainer to prevent debris being drawn up, and a foot valve to hold the water in the tube when the pump is not running, which eliminates the need for the pump to be primed every time it is turned on.

If the pump is housed in a chamber on a lower level than the base pool or reservoir there is no need to consider priming, as gravity will ensure that water constantly reaches the pump inlet. If the pump housing is higher than the pool, it should not be so high that it exceeds the suction capacity of the pump; this should be checked before the chamber is constructed. The suction pipe, one of the most important parts of the plumbing, should be of a strong, preferably reinforced material that will not collapse under the suction pressure. Flexible hosepipe should therefore be avoided.

Finally, it is important to ensure that all electrical connections near water are properly earthed. It is worth considering the addition of circuit breakers to give extra reassurance against electric shock, particularly with submersible pumps.

Alternative building materials

The advice on construction so far has assumed the use of liners for their versatility and ease of construction, particularly the material butyl, which in addition lasts a long time.

Watercourses are, however, frequently made in concrete alone, particularly where a great deal of rock work has to be incorporated. Without the waterproofing membrane underneath there is a greater risk of leaking, but provided that great care is taken and thorough use is made of the proprietary sealant compounds on the surface of the concrete, they can be very successful in

Left: A surface-mounted pump is suitable for systems in constant use

Above: A submersible pump is ideal for intermittant use and is easy to install

achieving a natural effect, particularly where attention is paid to the rough surfacing of the finish. Small cobbles or pebbles embedded into the surface of the concrete can also enhance the finished result, and give a more natural appearance, especially as algae will eventually clothe the uneven surfaces.

Some of the initial attempts to simulate watercourses and waterfalls in preformed fibreglass units were very difficult to integrate to give a natural effect. Although more recent forms have improved, in both their colouring and their structure, they still rely on heavy camouflaging at the sides to be acceptable. As with pools of fibreglass and other preformed materials, their rigidity makes waterside planting difficult, with plants requiring extra moisture, and one must resort to fast-growing, carpeting alpines that will tolerate dry conditions to creep over and cover the sides. Nevertheless, they have their attraction in their ease and speed of installation, requiring little skill and additional concreting. For small systems where good plant disguising is practised at the sides, they will bring the pleasure of moving water where alternatives may be too time-consuming or complex.

Landscaping

In many instances the excavated soil from a sunken pool is used to create raised areas for watercourses or rock gardens. On light soils much of this soil may be

Opposite: A mechanical fountain set in a small shallow pool

Right: This small formal pool incorporates a splashing fountain and a calmer area suitable for growing waterlilies

usable, but in most cases the soil is heavy subsoil which is unsuitable for good plant growth. It is most important not to spoil an informal water feature, which is dependent to a very large extent on the healthy growth of plants, by skimping on the quantity or the quality of soil to surround the feature. Insufficient quantity of soil often results in steep-sided mounds which look unnatural, and lack of organic matter and beneficial micro-organisms in subsoil or poor quality topsoil will result in very poor growth or death of plants. There is no hard and fast rule about the quantity of soil required in such features, but as a guideline when building up raised informal features the frontage of an artificial mound or raised area should not be less than three times the height.

Rock and water make good bedfellows in informal features, particularly watercourses and waterfalls. When choosing the type of rock there is a natural temptation to use Westmorland rock, with its beautiful fissuring and weatherworn appearance. Before succumbing to the temptation, consider the alternatives very carefully.

First, see if there is a good local stone, which may not only be very much cheaper but would also blend more successfully into the landscape. Westmorland is a very powerful stone of limestone origin, which when freshly quarried is often quite white. In a sandstone area, which may also contain an acid soil, limestone rocks could look quite incongruous and spoil one's attempts to recreate a natural landscape.

At all costs avoid making the watercourse in a steep-sided mound with too much rock in proportion to the space and height available. It would probably be far more effective and natural-looking to use the valuable rocks sparingly in outcrop form, particularly if some larger, flat pieces can be found. As already mentioned, avoid positioning the majority of the rocks directly alongside the watercourse in a form of ribbon development, tempting though this may be to disguise the edges of liner or concrete.

Outcrops of rock with minimal changes of height are more desirable than attempts to achieve a dramatic effect with a waterfall that is out of scale with the rest of the scheme. As with soil, there are no hard and fast rules on quantities in relation to areas, but in ordering rock ensure that the sizes vary, and if it is possible to be involved in the choice of pieces to be supplied, it is worth paying for that opportunity.

The positioning of the rocks should be considered as an integral part of the building of the watercourse and not the embroidery afterwards. On delivery each stone needs to be laid out and assessed for its suitability for the various situations. If pieces can be found from the outset suitable for the waterfalls without having to purchase additional flat pieces, this is a real bonus. The chances are, however, that these flat pieces will have to be sought specially, particularly where wide curtains of water in the waterfalls are required.

The rock work is a work of art, requiring a strong back, extreme patience, and attention to detail. One rock out of place, set at the wrong angle or sitting unnaturally can spoil the whole scheme; it is well worth seeking the help of a professional if large pieces of rock have been ordered.

Oxygenation There is one rewarding bonus on completion of the feature in addition to the aesthetic satisfaction. Once the water begins circulating there is an oxygenating and partial filtering effect on the water volume through the water's movement, particularly in the waterfalls. This has a direct benefit on any fish living in the base pool, and makes an indirect contribution to keeping the water clear.

GARDEN POOLS

In contrast to the noise and movement of fountains and watercourses, still water in pools gives restfulness and peace to a garden. A pool, in balance and harmony with the plant world, is difficult to resist in any setting, whether formal or informal, and becomes the basis of water gardening to the many home owners who have been lured by its attractions.

The size and character of many small gardens, particularly if a large area of patio has been incorporated, dictates a relatively formal approach to the pool shape. It is often far better to develop a strong formal pool, which can still house the majority of the plants associated with less rigid informal ponds, than to spoil the design by attempting a compromise that is neither natural looking nor strong in formal design.

Formal pools can be complemented very easily in small gardens by ornaments and containers, and in very small city gardens their strong shape, if linked to paths and walls, makes a superb setting for the softening effect of plants. They also make the perfect setting for the hybrid waterlilies, whose strong, bright summer colours are shown off to great advantage. On a purely practical note, the rectangular pool is one of the simplest shapes to construct and to surround with paving.

The irresistible appeal of water in its natural form may be the clue to the popularity of the informal kidney shape that epitomizes the pond of the majority of small gardens. Apart from its freedom of shape, if it is well constructed there is no hard line between the water's edge and the bog or moisture-loving plants that make a water feature so attractive and complete. While the formal pool can provide areas for the plants within the design, there is a special attraction created by a moist home at the water's edge for primulas, irises and many other moisture-loving plants. Such pools are ideal for plantsmen or plant collectors as they provide a wide range of conditions for plant growth. They are also very attractive to wildlife in the garden, offering a range of habitats that provide homes and food for a variety of animals and reptiles.

Siting

One of the greatest frustrations to the owners of small gardens is trying to establish a satisfactory compromise to meet the demands for space and provide adequate conditions for all the features they would like to include. Finding the right conditions for the site of a pool is no exception, and one frequently has to manage in totally alien surroundings.

Often the starting point for features in garden design may be the siting in relation to a much frequented window, and it would seem sensible to site a pool with this consideration as a major priority, particularly if one enjoys watching the wildlife which is inevitably drawn to its sides.

There are, however, other points to consider before making a decision about the precise site for the pool. First, the pool requires as much sunshine as possible if the planting is to flourish, particularly waterlilies, which are very shy of flowering in cold, shady sites. Second, avoid a site directly under trees, where the problem is not only shade but also the deposits of leaves and small twigs that fall into the pool and give off harmful methane gas during decomposition. Third, if possible avoid what seems to be the natural place to site a pool – the lowest point of the garden. There will be a possibility of waterlogging in this position, and if a liner has been used in the construction it may balloon up into the pool as a result of water pressure from underneath.

Finally, it is preferable if the pool is handy for electricity, a path system, and a water supply for topping up in the height of summer.

The freedom in an informal design to consider irregular and complex shapes has to be treated with great care. Good design frequently stems from a simple approach, and no medium illustrates this better than water. In finalizing the shape of the pool, it is a good idea to use a hosepipe to provide the outline, and assessing the shape from different viewpoints. As one of the major attractions of water is the opportunity to observe reflection on the water surface, the shape of the pool in relation to the main viewpoint has a considerable effect on the desired result. Such fine tuning is difficult to assess from a plan alone, and an old mirror on the ground in the proposed position can pinpoint whether a desired feature will later be reflected by the water.

Opposite: Plants are an essential part of any garden; *Dodecatheon meadia* (see page 105) is a particularly charming poolside plant

Right: *Primula vialii* (see page 114) has distinctive poker-like spikes of flowers

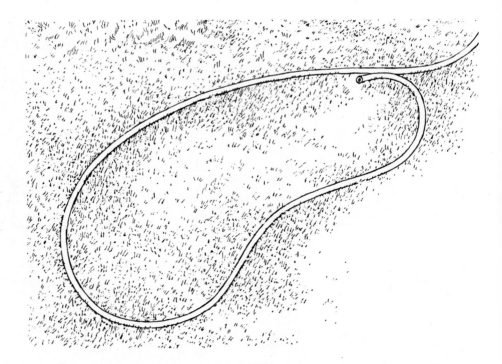

Lay a hosepipe on the lawn to check that the siting and the shape of the intended pool are satisfactory. It is important to view this from the main windows of the house

Keep the shape simple, and keep it wide in the line of the main viewpoint in order to see as much of the water surface as possible. From a constructional viewpoint a shape without too many fussy curves makes life much easier, particularly if using a liner, as will be explained later.

Although it is natural to consider water below the soil surface, with certain formal designs there are excellent opportunities to consider raised pools. Such features are ideally suited to formal patio areas, and can either be free-standing or link walls where small waterfalls or spouting ornaments may be attractive. They offer the advantage of bringing the water surface and planting closer to eye level, and dipping one's fingers into the pool becomes possible for the elderly and the very young with greater ease and safety.

Raised pools are frequently constructed using brick sidewalls, which can be given substantial coping to sit on at the water's edge. The limitations on size and depth given below are particularly important here in view of the greater risk of temperature variations above ground level.

Size

Although the size of the pool may be governed by limitations within the garden, it must be pointed out that the smaller the volume, the more difficult it becomes to achieve a successful balance of aquatic organisms to keep the water clear. A small pool is more subject to rapid and frequent fluctuations in temperature, which in turn stimulates rapid growth of algae and consequent greening. It is therefore recommended to have as large a pool as possible within the constraints of finance and design. Management aspects apart, a very small pool is limiting in the choice of planting possible, and unlike many other garden features it is not possible to change the shape or size very easily once it has been installed. If possible, consider the minimum size to be something in the region of 3.5–4.5 sq. m (40–50 sq. ft). In pools larger than this it becomes progressively easier to achieve the right balance in the water.

Depth

The depth of a pool is governed by the need to achieve a stable water temperature and the survival of plants and fish in the winter. The depth also affects the rate of growth of algae and consequent clouding. There is little point, however, in having a pool so deep that the extra depth serves no function. Assuming that the pool has been constructed with reasonably vertical side walls, the main area away from the marginal shelves needs to be approximately 45 cm (18 in) deep. Larger pools of over 9 sq. m (100 sq ft) would justify a depth of 60 cm (24 in), and 75 cm (30 in) is the maximum required even on a small lake.

It is a misconception to feel that a very deep pool is necessary for the survival of fish and to accommodate waterlilies. The main requirement in the winter time for fish survival is not so much the depth of water but the possibility of breathing unpolluted water. In order to achieve this, ice must not be allowed to seal the surface for long periods, which prevents the natural escape of methane gas. Most waterlilies will grow very successfully in 45 cm (18 in) of water, and benefit from the fact that the crowns are not so deep that they take a long time to warm up in the spring.

A half barrel makes a suitable container for a dwarf waterlily such as *Nymphaea pygmaea* 'Alba' and perhaps one of the less vigorous marginal plants

Construction materials

Having considered the factors affecting the style, site, shape and depth of pools, we are now in a position to consider aspects of construction. Apart from the ready made waterproof half-barrel, which can be a source of great pleasure as a miniature water garden, there are three main materials used in construction of water gardens: concrete, flexible liners and pre-moulded pools.

With the development of waterproof liners and their proven success over the last twenty years, it is tempting to discount concrete as an efficient method of holding water. There are, however, situations where its strength and texture or the availability of labour and materials make it a sensible choice. It has been superseded for various reasons. Considerable heavy manual effort is required in its use. Reinforcement needs to be considered with large pools. Rigid attention to detail is required throughout the construction process. In its raw state it is toxic to plants and fish and requires repeated initial filling and draining or treating with a sealant. It is prone to frost damage in extreme weather.

Opposite: An informal rock pool at the Royal Horticultural Society's garden at Wisley; a fine group of hostas are on the left

Below: Part of the water feature described on page 20. Waterproof liners allow greater versatility of design over moulded and concrete pools

Pool liners If there is one single factor which has led to the popularity of water gardening in the last two decades, it has been the development of waterproof membranes or pool liners, which give maximum flexibility in design and ease of construction. The three main types are made of synthetic rubber, plastic or polythene.

Polythene spearheaded the change from concrete to flexible liners. Its main weakness lay in its hardening and cracking when exposed to ultraviolet light. This hardened area inevitably occurred on the water line, where during the summer months evaporation caused the water level to drop an inch or two. The sun baked the polythene at this point and the inevitable cracking and consequent leaking occurred. Although the polythene could be covered with sand or stone to combat this weakness, on small ponds this attention to detail was not always given, and the vertical area just under the pool edge proved a difficult and critical zone to treat. Many pools then became unsightly, with ever-increasing bands of cracked polythene at the water's edge.

Superior grades of PVC soon superseded the polythene, as they were slower to break down under the influence of ultraviolet light. They have subsequently been strengthened by laminating techniques and a more recent reinforcing with nylon netting.

The ultimate development has been in the production of a rubberized sheet known as butyl. There are various grades, and for water garden purposes the minimum thickness should be .75 mm (0.030 in). Its matt black appearance makes it ideal for pond construction, giving the illusion of greater depth without garish colours. It is now widely used industrially, particularly in the lining of reservoirs, and has been found to be so superior to other lines that extensive guarantees are often given with the product. One of its many attributes is its ability to stretch into the pre-formed shapes created in the excavation for the pool, which eliminates many of the folds associated with the cheaper liners. There is no deterioration in ultraviolet light or frost, it can be

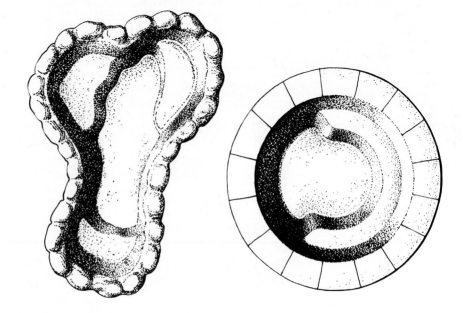

Premoulded pools come in a range of formal and informal shapes and sizes with prefabricated shallow planting ledges

prefabricated into intricate shapes, and should it be punctured accidentally with a garden fork can be repaired in much the same way as a cycle tyre puncture. With a minimum life expectancy of fifty years, it is a material second to none for pool construction.

Pre-moulded pools Pre-formed pools of plastic and fibreglass are offered in a variety of formal and informal shapes. They offer the ultimate in ready-made kits designed to catch the eye and make possible the installation of a pond in very little time. The fibreglass forms are strong, resistant to frost and ultraviolet damage, and have a good life expectancy. They can be very deceptive in size when seen standing vertically in sales displays, appearing to shrink dramatically when positioned in the ground.

They have their obvious limitations, and to the serious plantsman they are unlikely to be a first choice because of their mass-produced shapes. They have nevertheless brought the pleasure of a pool to countless thousands who would never have embarked upon such a feature if the work of concrete or the detail of liner design had had to be considered before purchase.

Construction using a liner In order to calculate the size of the liner required, one adds twice the pool's depth to the length and width of the pool required. A pool with overall dimensions of 2.75 by 2 m (9 by 6 ft) and a depth of 45 cm (18 in) will require a liner 3.75 by 2.75 m (12 by 9 ft). The pool can be of any shape that will fit into a rectangle of 2.75 by 2 m (9 by 6 ft). With materials that do not have the stretch properties of butyl it would be sensible to add a further 30 cm (1 ft) foot to the length and breadth for overlap. With butyl, however, this is not necessary.

As mentioned on page 38, when considering the shape of the pool the length and breadth measurements are best checked by making the outline of the pool on the proposed site, first with a hosepipe and then, when the shape and size have been decided on, by using sand to record the outline when the hose is removed.

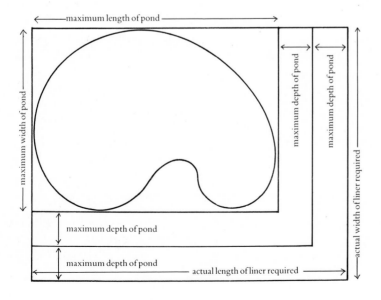

This diagram shows the measurements needed to calculate the area of liner required for a pool

The first step in excavating a pool is to cut just inside the line previously marked out

Dig out the soil, making the pool sides slope at a slight angle, leaving marginal shelves about 23 cm (9 in) wide, checking levels as you dig. You may wish to reinforce these shelves with concrete if the soil is crumbly

The excavation is now complete. In this instance much of the excess soil has been piled up to form a watercourse and rock garden. It is a good idea to press a layer of damp sand over the surface so no sharp stones pierce the liner

Drape the liner over the excavated pool, ensuring that the overlap is even all round

Place rocks around the edge of the liner to keep it in position. As the pool fills with water the rocks should be moved to ensure the liner fits snugly

When the pool is full the surplus lining should be trimmed to about 15 cm (6 in). This flap is then covered with soil, stones or a formal pool edging depending on which is required

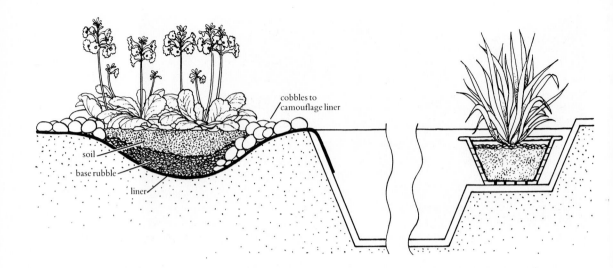

cobbles to
camouflage liner

soil

base rubble

liner

A bog garden can be created by extending the liner beyond the pool edge to create a shallow depression. Bog plants can be planted directly into the soil, which being at the same level as the water in the pool is kept permanently moist

For the serious plantsman interested in the range of waterside plants grown in bog conditions, it is at this stage that consideration should be given to an adjacent bog garden. If the liner size is enlarged accordingly to include the bog area, the division between water and soil area can be made with rocks or large stones. The bog area can be filled with base rubble and then soil to a few inches above the water level, so the plants are not waterlogged but can push their roots into the water as required.

The opportunity to create this bog effect is one of the advantages of using liners rather than prefabricated pools in informal areas. All too frequently one sees moisture-loving plants planted on the outside edge of fibreglass or lined pools where they have no more moisture than in any other part of the garden. One of the joys of informal water gardening lies in the blending of several groups of plants with a varying dependence on water. If this is considered at the design stage, and allowance made for the bog plants, it can make a significant impact on the appearance of the water feature.

Pool excavation

To excavate the pool, begin cutting out just inside the line previously marked out with sand or hosepipe, on the inside edge as it is always easier to enlarge the hole than to reduce it. Dig out, making the pool sides slope at a slight angle, which will both reduce the risk of the sides crumbling as you progress and later will help the liner to settle onto the mould as the weight of water stretches it down. A further advantage of sloped sides is noticed when severe frost is experienced, as the expansion of the ice is less damaging.

In most cases it is desirable to create a shelf around the perimeter of the pool some 23 cm (9 in) deep and 23 cm (9 in) wide. It will provide a platform to house the containers holding marginal plants. After creating the shelf continue digging and shaping the edges at a slight angle until the desired depth is reached, normally about 45 cm (18 in).

If the surface soil is so crumbly that the edges fall away, some form of reinforcing the surface area around the pool perimeter should be considered before further excavation takes place. A shallow layer of concrete is one method of doing this, which later can provide a strong base for any future edging stones which may surround the water.

A constant check should be made on surface levels using a straight edge and spirit level. Any adjustments are best made at this stage, before adding the liner, by building up the soil on the lower side.

When the required depth and shape have been achieved it is advisable to cover as much as possible of the exposed surface with dampened sand, particularly the pool bottom, to buffer the effect of any sharp stones that may not have been spotted and removed on excavation. There is a polyester matting available for this job on very stony ground. The advantage of the polyester is its longevity, a point to bear in mind if tempted to use cheap alternatives like newspaper, which after rotting away leaves the liner exposed to the stones.

The hole is now ready for the liner to be inserted. The liner itself should have been left unfolded on a nearby lawn to absorb any heat and make it more flexible to use. Stretch the liner over the pool loosely, and anchor with heavy stones around the sides before starting to fill with water. As the weight of the water on the butyl increases it will stretch into the shape of the pool, reducing the creases which will occur on complex shapes. The anchor stones can be removed when it is noticed that most of the tension has been released and the weight of the water is being taken by the subsoil. There should be a flap of 15 cm (6 in) or more remaining around the edges, either for covering and cementing under the paving edging stones or to disguise into the surrounding soil.

In most pools, particularly formal pools, it is valuable to underpin these paving edges with bricks or decorative walling stone. If these supports are laid on top of the liner there is the advantage not only of increased rigidity to the paving edge, but also the unattractive 'tide mark' on the liner as the water level drops in the summer is not seen. Paying attention to detail in this edging, particularly the measures that ensure that the water level reaches as near as possible the top edge of the paving stones, makes all the difference to the finished result.

Before the excitement of planting begins, two further points are worth mentioning. First, before finishing the surface of the paving round the edge it is useful to incorporate conduit or a length of waterproof electric cable under the paving for later installations of accessories such as heaters or pumps. Second, if the pool is fairly large it may be easier to plant some of the deep marginals, oxygenators, and waterlilies which occupy positions near the centre before the pool is fully filled with water, when handling and moving about becomes more difficult.

3
Looking after the Pool

ALGAE AND ALGICIDES

Algae are simple microscopic plants, with over a hundred different species common to aquatic environments. Their presence causes more concern in water garden management than any other single problem, and a considerable range of products has been introduced for their removal. In the section devoted to filtration, their long-term control by starving out their food supply is discussed.

There are related forms of algae which, unlike the common free-floating uni-cellular forms, have a filamentous structure forming cottonwool-like masses of green growth. These algae are known as blanketweed, and their presence is nearly always associated with pools containing crystal-clear water. Its control in small pools requires diligent hand weeding, particularly in the spring, by means of a forked stick twirled in the weed and netted out. In large pools, where this is impracticable, the product Algimycin can be applied at the rate of 30 ml to 1130 litres (1 fl. oz to 250 gal) of water. Wherever possible, remove heavy growth of blanketweed before applying the chemical, as large quantities of decaying algae can reduce the oxygen content of the water, and avoid direct application on aquatic plants. Several applications may be necessary where infestation is heavy.

For the more common single-celled algae, where it is not possible to use filtration as a control measure, one has to resort to the use of algicides, diluted from a bottle and poured straight into the pool. A simple chemical remedy is permanganate of potash, mixed at the rate of $\frac{1}{4}$ tsp for every 900 litres (200 gal) of water, dissolved in 2.2 litres ($\frac{1}{2}$ gal). When dissolving the crystals, take care not to splash the concentrate on hands and clothes; the resulting stain on one's hands has only one remedy for its removal – time! Introduce small quantities of the concentrate in various parts of the pool for more even distribution. When required the concentrate can be spread across a wider pool by means of pushing and pulling a yard broom across the water's surface.

A form of biological control worth trying is to introduce quantities of *Daphnia*, small water fleas which feed on free-floating algae as their main diet. These crustaceans are sold as fish food, so they are only effective in fish-free pools, and their effect is only temporary.

It must be stressed that algicides do not change the conditions that encourage algae to flourish. Frequent applications are required to maintain the improve-ment, and there is always the temptation to overdo dosage rates in an attempt to hasten the process, risking damage to plant and fish life.

While the problem of cloudy water is most frequently associated with algae, there are certain conditions that cause cloudiness where algicides have little or no effect. In a newly planted pool, for example, the organic matter brought in with the planting soil contains fine particles that are released into the water in suspension. Such a condition, while unattractive in early establishment, is quickly overcome, and within a few days the water clears. In an established pond, where large fish frequently disturb the muddy sediment and plant root

Opposite: An informal pool with floating duckweed

zone, a flocculating agent such as Acurel causes the fine particles to run together and sink to the bottom. Where this disturbance by the fish is likely to continue, steps should be taken to remove bottom sediment and cover exposed soil and roots with large gravel.

Other algicides worthy of mention include Algizin, which has a broad band of control to include fungal infections of fish, and there are pond blocks which slowly dissolve in the water. Their mode of action is similar to a slow release fertilizer, dissolving the algicide over a long period. One block is normally adequate for 1100 litres (250 gal) of water, but in alkaline conditions the block dissolves more slowly and is weaker in action. If conditions are very murky, it may be used at the rate of one block to 450 litres (100 gal) but there is some risk of young waterlily plants being weakened.

FILTRATION

Where it is difficult to achieve the required levels of plant life in a pool, and particularly where stocking with large fish is to be considered, a form of filtration will be required to keep the water clear. A filter will not only remove the visible waste products such as debris and faeces, but also the invisible ammonia and carbon dioxide that support the offending floating algae. Frequently algaecides are recommended for killing the floating algae, but as they are only a short-term remedy and present a possible hazard to plant life, it is better to consider long-term filtration, which will have the effect of starving the algae out.

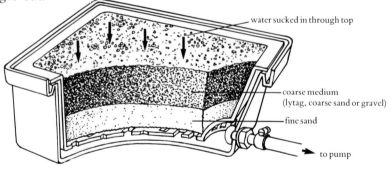

water sucked in through top

coarse medium
(lytag, coarse sand or gravel)

fine sand

to pump

Above: A simple submerged filter unit can be attached to a submersible pump. This system is suitable for small patio pools

Right: A sophisticated external biological filter suitable for pools with high fish populations

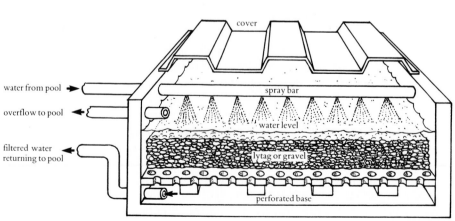

cover

water from pool →

overflow to pool ←

spray bar

water level

filtered water returning to pool ←

lytag or gravel

perforated base

A simple pool filter recirculates the pool water through a container of filter medium either at the bottom of the pool itself or in a separate filter chamber, preferably above water level. There are two basic types of filter.

Submersible filters often take the form of a kit attachment for the inlet of a pump that also drives a waterfall or fountain. They have the advantage of being hidden under water, are cheap and easy to install, and require no external space for installation. They are, however, less efficient than external filters, and are particularly prone to clogging by excess debris. If the pump is not used continuously they are more prone to deterioration by being under water, and are frequently inactivated where algicides or fish medicines are applied to the pool.

There are two kinds of external filter. Gravity fed filters enable water to be drawn through the filter medium, causing efficient straining of debris. Elevated filters are situated above pool level, enabling water to be pumped into them from above, which provides much better aeration. Their positioning and consequent screening must be considered at the outset of the water garden design, as in a large pool the filter system can be quite extensive. Filtration occurs in two forms: mechanical filtration, when debris is drawn through the filter medium, and biological filtration, when dissolved wastes are absorbed. The latter system becomes more efficient if the filtration medium used provides a large surface area on which bacteria can grow, and the following materials are recommended.

Lytag or other lightweight aggregates These materials are widely used in horticulture, particularly in hydroculture or for use on greenhouse benches. Being porous, the granules provide a large surface area for the growth of bacteria in the many crevices. It is light in weight, clean to handle, and unlikely to damage liners if introduced into a pool.

Foam The properties of foam in providing a large surface area make it an ideal material for physical filtration, particularly as a pre-filter to extract fine debris before biological filtration. Some polystyrene foams contain fire retardant chemicals, however, which can be toxic.

Sand Care must be taken in the choice of sand from the wide variety available. Research into the use of sand for surface drainage of sports turf has shown that there are only a few sand types with uneven particle size which do not compress easily and thus keep a free, open structure for bacterial growth. These sands are mainly found in the Bedfordshire area and are much sought after. Ordinary builder's sand will tend to clog the filter.

Gravel There are many types of gravel, most of which are suitable for bacterial growth. The ideal gravels are those with a small particle size and a rough surface, rather than the shiny pea gravels. All gravels are heavy, and for large external filters the weight may make this medium impracticable.

It is possible to construct a series of such filters with water pumped through progressively smaller particle sizes. If such a system of biological filtration is to

be successful, the system should be considered as a living organism in its own right, requiring adequate levels of oxygen. If the pool has methods of increasing absorbed oxygen through features like fountains and waterfalls, this is advantageous; alternatively, if the pumped water falls onto the filter chamber from a wide-necked pipe outlet, oxygen is introduced into the water at that point.

If fish are present in the pool, harmful ammonia and urea are produced from their excreta and from the decomposition of any uneaten food. Ammonia will be converted into toxic nitrites, and later into non-toxic nitrates by the bacteria in the filter if sufficient oxygen is present. If there is adequate plant life in the pool, the end product of filtration – nitrates – are removed by the plants.

Once in operation, filters must be kept running continuously, as a break of only a few days may cause other bacteria to produce toxic hydrogen sulphide. Biological filtration continues even at very low temperatures, and if the filter is stopped harmful bacteria replace the beneficial ones and the filter medium must be thoroughly cleaned before restarting. The full effect of a filter may take several weeks, and sometimes months, to show, but it will prove well worth the effort when the pool becomes noticeably more clear again.

The effectiveness of a filtration system will be influenced by the size and type of pump. In the case of a submersed filter the pump will need to draw a quarter of the total volume of water through each hour. For the ultimate in filtration, for example in Koi pools, an external filter size should be one eighth the volume of the pool, requiring a flow rate of 90 litres per minute per cubic metre of filter medium (flow rate of 1000 gal per hour per cu yd of filter medium) to allow adequate aeration. As a guideline, 1 cu m of medium will support 27 kg (1 cu yd for 50 lb) of fish.

WATER ACIDITY OR ALKALINITY (pH)

Understanding the principle of water acidity is as important in the management of a water garden as the choice of suitable plants is for an acid garden. In a pool adequately stocked with plants and no fish, the reabsorption of carbon dioxide into the water presents no serious problem. If, however, the pool is heavily stocked with fish, the excess production of carbon dioxide can cause the water to have a low pH reading. The pH scale is a measure used in assessing the degree of acidity or alkalinity in water or soils, and has a neutral reading of 7.0. Readings above 7 are alkaline, and those below 7 acid. There are seldom readings below 5 except in peat bogs; similarly, it is unusual fo find higher alkaline readings than 8.5, though the scale runs from 0 to 14.

Several factors can influence the pH of a pond: rainfall, water changes and the action of plants. In areas of hard water it can be expected that on initial filling the pH reading would be quite high. It is therefore recommended not to change the pool water in one operation so as to avoid a drastic change to the pH reading and the consequent upsetting of the biological balance. There have been cases where lime has been applied in an attempt to cure a cloudy pool, and when applied in one heavy dose the resultant chemical change was so drastic that it caused considerable distress to the inhabitants of the pool.

Opposite: It is important not to introduce too many fish into a small pool, otherwise nitrate levels will build up and oxygen will be in short supply

The pH level affects the way in which certain chemicals exist in water, particularly ammonia, which in its free state is quite toxic, while as an ammonium salt is much less toxic. Ideally, slightly alkaline water, about pH 7.0–7.5, should be aimed for, and once achieved, maintained without serious fluctuation. It is advisable where valuable fish are stocking the pond to monitor the pH periodically with a simple pH test kit.

POND LIFE

A pond contains an abundant plant life together with a varied animal population, ranging from single-celled protozoans to vertebrates. Some are carnivores, and other feed directly on plants. As with the plants, many animals are not primarily aquatic; they have adopted water as their habitat and are known as secondary aquatic animals, and include some snails, mites, about eleven orders of insects, and the water spider.

Water can be said to provide four well defined areas in which pond animals live according to their particular way of life: the water surface, the open water, the vegetation area and the mud at the bottom.

Some common inhabitants of the pool:
1 frog
2 frogspawn
3 great ramshorn snail
4 water boatman
5 great diving beetle
6 caddis fly larva
7 dragonfly nymph
8 great pond snail
9 dragonfly
10 pond skater

As a result of tension existing on the water surface, many small animals are supported both above and below this skin. Those living on the surface and feeding on dead and dying insects include pond skaters, water crickets and the water measurer. Skimming the surface but sometimes descending below are whirligig beetles. Animals using the underside of the tension film for support when taking in air include the larvae and pupae of some flies, such as gnats and mosquitoes. In the centre of ponds, away from the bank and marginal plants, live the fish and the planktonic crustaceans such as water fleas. Perhaps the largest number of easily seen animals live in the vegetation area. The herbivores include the larvae of the caddis fly, caterpillars of the china-mark moths and water snails. The carnivores include the nymphs of dragonflies and damsel flies, several species of water beetle such as the great diving beetle (a very voracious species preying on any small pond creature), water bugs, including the water boatman and water scorpion, and several species of leech. Although only a few species live in the mud at the bottom of ponds, because of the shortage of oxygen, it supports quite a large population including the 'blood worm' larvae of midges.

In addition to the permanent inhabitants, other animals are attracted to ponds either to drink, to feed or to clean themselves. These include grass snakes in search of frogs and fish, water shrews hunting for insects, and water voles feeding on the marginal plants. Moorhens will nest in the reeds, swallows hunt for insects over the water, house martins collect mud for their nests, and kingfishers and herons hunt for fish. Bats, too, enjoy hunting near water.

4
Planting the Pool

Before deciding what to plant in the wide range of conditions offered by the environment of a pool, there are certain basic principles to be considered. The most important of these relates to the planting of the inside of the pool itself, and the effect this planting has on the condition of the water.

In most clear ponds there is an extensive covering of surface leaf, often provided by free-floating plants. A priority in planting is to ensure from the beginning that a high proportion of submerged and surface-leaved plants are planted and maintained. No matter how imaginative and successful the marginal and waterside planting is, its effect will be spoilt by cloudy or dirty water, and avoiding this condition should be paramount in practical considerations.

The condition of clear water is known as a 'good balance', and it is achieved by the reduction of microscopic algae, present in heavy numbers in water where there is good light and mineral salts on which to feed. The successful early establishment of plants is crucial to creating a good balance, particularly if there is a period of hot, sunny weather soon after the pool is constructed and filled. The rapid greening that can take place under these conditions often leads pool owners to drain and refill their pools, mistakenly believing that the clouding was as a result of dirt. Refrain from this draining, as clouding is almost impossible to prevent in freshly filled pools at the height of summer when the plant life has not had a chance to become established.

Two types of plants need to be introduced at the beginning: surface-leaved plants and oxygenating plants. These reduce the algae in two ways. First, the surface-leaved plants reduce the amount of light, on which the algae depend. Second, by absorbing mineral salts themselves they help to starve out the food source of the algae. They also have other roles, particularly the submerged plants which oxygenate the water, provide food and spawning areas for fish, and support many tiny beneficial organisms. Waste products produced by fish are in turn absorbed by the plants and converted into plant proteins. This process is helpful to both fish and plants, preventing the build-up of toxic ammonia.

Reduction of surface light is an important part of the planting strategy, though total cover of the water surface would do more harm than good by blocking out too much of the surface light. Between half and two-thirds of the surface area should be covered by leaves of either surface floating plants or submerged plants such as waterlilies. Obviously this cover is almost impossible to provide on a newly established pond; until the other plants become established, for very small ponds one may have to resort to more surface floating plants than will later be required, netting out the excess in later weeks.

Having decided to introduce both surface-leaved and oxygenating plants, there remains the question of how to plant them under water. The most obvious answer may appear to be that one should provide a thick layer of soil on the bottom of the pond and around the marginal shelves and plant into this soil.

Opposite: Hostas, primulas and ferns by the poolside

There may be a case for this method in a pool of native plants where a natural effect is intended, but in an ornamental pool such a system is in danger of becoming unmanageable, as vigorous species will spread rapidly, swamping the smaller plants. Subsequent removal or propagation of a plant becomes more difficult in this free-for-all system, necessitating substantial disturbance of the pool bottom and disentanglement of root systems.

It is preferable to plant into perforated plastic containers known as planting crates, which constrict the vigorous species to their designated space. They are made in a variety of sizes and have wide, flat bases to help stability under water. Ordinary plastic pots are not as successful for this purpose; the plants appear to prefer the mesh sides for greater gaseous movement. The compost used in the crates need be no more than good, clean garden soil, free of organic matter and quick-acting fertilizers, which encourage algae growth. If fertilizer is added it should be of a slow-release type, releasing nutrients over a long period of time in small quantities.

The planting technique in the crate is exactly the same as for planting or potting normal plants, avoiding too shallow or too deep planting. A half-inch layer of gravel should be added over the surface, which will prevent fish from disturbing the soil in the crate. Where suitable soil is short, many of the submerged plants are able to survive in gravel alone, as their food is mainly absorbed from the water through their leaves. Further information on planting depths and special requirements is given in the detailed descriptions of plants (see page 79 onwards).

Generally the planting of aquatic plants takes place between April and September, and where this coincides with hot, sunny weather ensure that the submerged plants are not out of the water for longer than is absolutely necessary, as severe shrivelling occurs on exposure to sunshine and air. If plants ordered by post arrive at an inconvenient time and some delay is likely before planting, insert the plants into buckets or containers of water as a temporary measure rather than leaving them in plastic bags, where sweating and rotting may occur in hot weather.

OXYGENATING PLANTS

These submerged plants, resembling bunches of water weed, are the first group to be planted in the new pool. They are sold as bunches of unrooted cuttings about 23 cm (9 in) long, nipped together at their base by a small piece of lead. The lead helps to prevent their floating in the water if they are loosened after planting. The bunches are inserted into holes made in the compost in the planting crates and firmed in, in much the same way that seedlings are pricked out into seedboxes. Plant the bunches firmly, as they are likely to be nibbled at and dislodged by fish. This interest in, and possible damage to, the plants is one reason why it is recommended to introduce fish only when the planting has become established.

A medium-sized planting crate, measuring 25 cm (10 in) square and 15 cm (6 in) deep will hold six bunches of oxygenators; as a general guideline, five bunches should be planted for every square metre (or one bunch per sq ft) of water. It certainly will do no harm to exceed this figure, ensuring a more rapid

Several bunches of unrooted shoots of oxygenating plants weighted with small pieces of lead can be inserted into planting crates

lead weights

build-up, and provided that they are planted in crates they can easily be controlled later if they become out of hand. They should not be planted deeper than 90–120 cm (3–4 ft), and thrive between 45 and 60 cm (18 and 24 in). Try to mix the plants, as some, such as the starwort (*Callitriche autumnalis*) continue to oxygenate throughout the winter, while others, such as the hornwort (*Ceratophyllum demersum*), prove less attractive to fish that nibble at young growth, and would be useful to plant where fish are already present. There are many submerged plants that act as oxygenators, but only about half a dozen are normally sold specifically for the purpose. These are: *Ceratophyllum demersum* (hornwort), *Crassula helmsii, Eleocharis acicularis* (hair grass), *Elodea canadensis* (Canadian pondweed), *Fontinalis antipyretica* (willow moss), *Lagarosiphon major, Myriophyllum verticillatum* (water milfoil), and *Ranunculus aquatilis* (water crowfoot). For futher details about these plants see page 100.

WATERLILIES (NYMPHAEA)

There are approximately fifty hardy and tropical species of waterlily now gracing the pools and lakes of northern Europe, and the dozens of the more popular and colourful hybrids owe their existence to a small band of dedicated hybridists from the mid-nineteenth century onwards. One name stands out from this small band, that of the Frenchman Joseph Bory Latour-Marliac. Before his time only the white-flowered *N. alba* was grown outside. With great patience he set about obtaining colourful hardy hybrids by carefully cross-pollinating *N. alba* with several tropical species. After years of failure, he succeeded, in the late 1870s, and introduced *Nymphaea × marliacea* 'Rosea', a very popular hybrid to this day. Nearly seventy new hybrids followed, including *N. × marliacea* 'Chromatella', and in 1883 many of the *N. × laydekeri* hybrids, called after his son-in-law Maurice Laydeker. Such were the demands for his exotic new colours in hardy waterlilies that he set up a commercial nursery in Temple-sur-Lot in the south of France.

Marliac was extremely evasive about both his methods and the parentage of his hybrids and unfortunately on his death in 1911 his secrets died with him. Few new forms have been introduced since then, though his grandson, M. Jean Laydeker, a distinguished plant collector and horticulturist, continued the family business and interest in plants.

There are two types of basal growth of waterlilies: the native *N. alba* is an example of those with thick tuberous rootstocks which increase from 'eyes' or side pieces; the other type is derived from *N. tuberosa* and the American *N. odorata* which have long, fleshy rhizomes. Both types contain an infinite range of flower colours, though blue remains elusive to the hybridists of the hardy species.

Opposite: *Myriophyllum verticillatum*, the water millfoil, is an oxygenating plant (see page 100)

Right: *Nymphaea × marliacea* 'Carnea' (see also page 90)

Waterlilies are not as demanding as commonly supposed, most of them being happy to grow in water 45–60 cm (18–24 in) deep. There are many that will flourish in very shallow water and barrels, where they look superb. They require full sun and a good, rich soil free of material that may rot down and later pollute the water. They do not like water movement or turbulence, and although they will tolerate certain small domestic fountains they are at their best in completely still and quiet water. This association with quiet may be the reason why Harpocrates, the Greek god of silence, wore waterlilies round his head.

It is tempting to fill the pool with as many waterlilies as possible, but they look far better when occupying between a third and a half of the pool's surface. If more than one colour is to be planted, choose colours that will blend harmoniously. When planting, identify which type of rootstock the plant has. The rhizomatous root should be planted horizontally just under the surface of the compost, with the crown just protruding from the soil; the thicker, tuberous rootstocks, with their fringe of fibrous roots just under the crown, should be planted vertically in the compost, again with the top of the crown just protruding.

Planting crates are suitable, using the largest size or special waterlily crate for the medium to vigorous plants; the soil must be changed every second to third year. When planting, remove old leaves, fibrous roots and any damaged or diseased areas. Firm the compost really well around the rootstock and cover the compost with a 1 cm ($\frac{1}{2}$ in) layer of gravel. Submerge initially to a depth where the young leaves can reach the surface almost immediately, by underpinning the

Planting a waterlily in a basket. The layer of gravel will deter fish from grubbing around the rootstocks

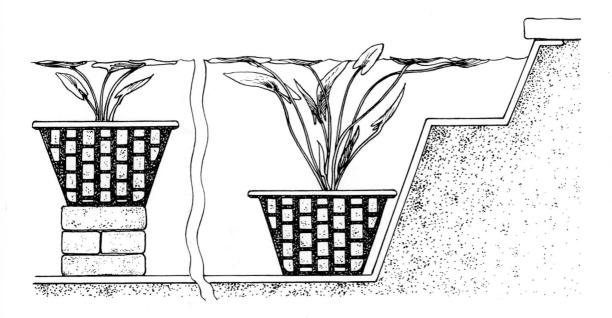

planting crate with bricks so that there is about 20 cm (8 in) of water above the crate. After two to three weeks growth should be strong enough to lower the planting crate to its final position at the bottom of the pond. For larger ponds and the very vigorous species and hybrids of waterlily, special containers or large boxes about 60–90 cm (2–3 ft) square are made on the pool bottom, and the water is introduced gradually after planting as the leaves grow.

In order to help the establishment of newly planted waterlilies, their planting crates should be raised up from the pool bottom on bricks. As the plant grows the crate can be lowered until it sits on the bottom

For the first few weeks in the summer after planting, the size and colour of the flowers and leaves may be disappointing, but in the second year the plant will have recovered enough vigour almost to double in size. No firm guide can be given to the number of waterlilies that can be planted in relation to pool size, as each one varies in vigour, but the classification of vigour given in the lists of recommended plants will offer a clue to the quantities possible to grow. Every three to four years the crowns may need to be divided; this need is indicated by the leaves being thrust above the water rather than lying flat on the surface. Division of the crowns should if possible be undertaken in May or June; the crowns are lifted, and the side shoots of the main rhizome removed and replanted.

OTHER SUBMERGED PLANTS WITH SURFACE–FLOATING LEAVES

Although waterlilies are highlighted as the main surface-leaved plant used in pools, there are a small number of ornamental genera that provide additional interest and lengthen the flowering season. Their planting is very similar to that of waterlilies; their particular characteristics and requirements are given in the plant lists (see page 101). These plants include: *Aponogeton distachyos*, *Nuphar* spp., *Nymphoides peltatum* var. *bennettii*, and *Orontium aquaticum*.

MARGINAL PLANTS

The planting described so far has been desirable, if not essential, to establish clear water and maintain its balance. The group of plants referred to as marginals qualify for their inclusion on more aesthetic grounds. While there is tremendous strength in the lines of a pool containing only horizontal surface foliage, it would be limited to a fairly short flowering season and a rather stark appearance. Marginal plants not only soften the edges of pools and streams with their contrasting styles of growth, they also provide additional summer colour, even early spring colour with the marsh marigolds, and provide homes for many insects and small creatures which require the cover of dense, upright foliage.

They are called marginals because they are happiest in the marginal areas around pools where the water is shallower. The small ornamental pool is normally made with a shelf to contain the plants, which may be planted either in aquatic crates, or directly onto soil-filled shelves about 23 cm (9 in) deep. When a planting crate sits on this shelf there is approximately 8–15 cm (3–6 in) of water above the crown of the plant, which allows the majority of marginals to grow quite comfortably. Plants have their own optimum planting depth (in aquatic terms this relates to the depth of the water above the crown, not the depth of planting under the surface of the compost), which are listed with the plant descriptions. If the shelf is a standard 23 cm (9 in) deep the depth can again be varied by putting bricks or individual plinths under the planting crates where shallower depths are required. Many of the plants defined as marginals may stray to deeper water or onto drier banks, as they are able to adapt between aquatic and moist environments; these are better confined singly to planting crates to prevent their spreading and mixing with slower growing neighbours.

Opposite: *Primula florindae* (see page 113) with *Gunnera manicata* in the background (see page 105)

Right: *Iris laevigata*, one of the finest aquatic plants for early summer (see page 84)

A typical example of such a spreader is *Glyceria aquatica*, an attractive, vigorous grass which is at home in shallow water or moist banks. Allow it freedom to spread and in no time it becomes a nightmare to control. There are several like it, and with no check to their growth through lack of water unrestricted planting must be considered with great care.

Marginals are, however, a beautiful group of plants, making a pool complete both in formal and informal designs. Taller specimens run the risk of being blown over on windy sites if planted in small planting crates, so a method of stabilizing the crates under water must be devised. They bring a luxuriant freshness to the garden, helping to protect the surface of the water from wind, and in some cases provide partial shade. It is hard to imagine a pool without this group of plants, which are not demanding in their requirements for soil as their vigorous growth needs little encouragement. A clean, heavy loam, free of decomposing material, is all that is necessary. The choice of material is governed by the scale of the landscaping and the blending of colours and textures.

There are certain plants, referred to as deep marginals, where the standard 23 cm (9 in) ledge would be too shallow. These are vigorous species that would be better planted in water of 30 cm (12 in) or more, either on a deeper portion of shelf or in deeper water away from the margin.

SURFACE–FLOATING PLANTS

There are two forms of floating plants: the floating carpeting plants and those that are individual floaters. They have enormous value in light reduction, and many are attractive. There can be problems with introducing the carpeting forms into larger pools, as once introduced they may take over and prove difficult, if not impossible, to eradicate. On very small pools, however, there is no reason why they should not be considered as a means of reducing light, removing mineral salts from the water, and providing shelter for fish fry and other minute creatures.

They can simply be dropped onto the water surface, and in warm, sunny weather multiply rapidly. Many survive by overwintering bodies on the bottom of the pool which resurface in the spring. One such plant, *Azolla*, can spread so tightly on the surface that the pool gives no indication of water. Many accidental steps have been taken into small pools in such a condition, to the great enjoyment and amusement of onlookers! (Such pools can, of course, be a danger to small children.) Further information on this group will be found under *Azolla*, *Lemna* and *Pistia* (carpeting floaters); *Eichhornia*, *Hydrocharis*, *Stratiotes* and *Trapa* (individual floaters).

MOISTURE–LOVING PLANTS

This group of plants complements the water planting if there is an area of permanently moist but not waterlogged soil, either at the side of the pool or nearby. In the section on the construction of a pool (see page 000) the inclusion of a raised wet area at the poolside for such planting was suggested. If space permits, it is nevertheless much better to construct a moisture garden in its own right, with a separate liner, where there is not a waterlogged layer at the base and the area does not need to be raised up for the aeration of the soil. A separate moisture or bog garden is relatively easy and cheap to construct, as it does not require the careful treatment of the edges of the waterproofing medium as is required in pool construction, as these edges are simply disguised by topsoil.

A very simple system involves using the very cheapest form of liner available (even a damaged one) which could be polythene or plastic as it will not be exposed to ultraviolet light, and it does not have to be completely waterproof. The topsoil is excavated to a depth of about 38–45 cm (15–18 in) and the soil stored nearby as it will be returned after inserting the liner. Before the liner is positioned holes or slits are made in it so that very slow drainage or seepage can occur after installation. The edges of the liner need only be 30–35 cm (12–14 in) below the final soil level. It is useful to insert a length of hose before returning the topsoil. It should also be slitted or punctured at regular intervals, sealed at one end and with a connector at the other, so that topping up with water in dry weather is made a simple operation. The soil is then returned, adequately improved with ample organic matter, covering the sides of the liner.

This system and the extended marginal shelf described on page 48 now allows the range of moisture-loving plants to be included, instead of being limited to the hard and often dry margins associated with lined pools.

ROCK AND DRY SOIL PLANTING

The soil is likely to be dry around the edges of fibreglass pools, and it is better to plant subjects that will enjoy these conditions in preference to the moisture lovers, which will not be at home. The list given here is not exhaustive, but will be a useful guide to plants that can cover and soften these areas rapidly:

Acaena buchananii
Ajuga reptans
Alyssum saxatile
Arabis caucasica
Aubretia species and cultivars
Calluna species and cultivars
Campanula poscharskyana
Dianthus deltoides
Dryas octapetala
Erica species and cultivars
Euonymus fortunei
Hebe pinguifolia
Hedera species and cultivars
Hypericum olympicum
Iberis sempervirens
Mentha requienii
Phlox subulata and cultivars
Thymus serpyllum
Veronica prostrata
Vinca species and cultivars

5
Seasonal Work in the Water Garden

Spring

If necessary, formal pools can be thoroughly cleaned out in early spring and waterlilies divided and planted in fresh soil. Otherwise, just remove any excess build-up of decaying vegetation. Where this has occurred, provide a partial water change (a third to a half of the water volume) to remove the absorbed toxic materials.

Feed fish as soon as they become active and inspect them for any sign of disease or parasites. Keep a weather eye open for herons at this time of the year.

If a pond has a population of frogs it will be noticed that the tadpoles actively assist in the spring clean-up of old organic remains.

Opposite: Male and female common (or smooth) newts. The male is in breeding dress. Remember when cleaning up the pool that newts lay their eggs in blanketweed

Left: The pool in spring

SUMMER

Divide plants as required, particularly material that has become invasive. New planting can be carried out. Divide waterlilies where the foliage is being thrust vertically above the water surface. Remove any leaves that show early signs of infection with pests and diseases, particularly the leaf-mining midge before it has a chance to skeletonize leaves. If a specialized form of filamentous algae known as blanketweed starts to make its appearance (always in very clear water), insert a broom handle and rotate among the weed to draw it out.

However, do remember that newts will lay their eggs in blanketweed, which will also provide a natural shelter for the young of both newts and fish. Some pool owners may therefore wish to retain a patch of this 'weed'.

In thundery weather fish may suffer from lack of oxygen. This problem can be overcome by allowing water from a hosepipe to splash into the pond and agitate the water.

AUTUMN

Prune hard the excess growth of submerged planting – this will only die later and help to choke the bottom. Remove any decomposing material. Provide a partial water change, as recommended in spring. Remove the pump if fitted and replace with a water heater. Cover the water surface with netting if heavy leaf fall is experienced over the water. Feed fish to build them up for the winter months.

If reed mace (*Typha*) or water plantain (*Alisma*) is present then their flowering stems may be usefully taken for use in dried flower arrangements, remembering to spray the reed mace with hair lacquer to prevent its exploding seed dispersal in spring. Remove ripe seed pods of plants such as *Iris pseudacorus* before the seeds fall since they may germinate freely where not required.

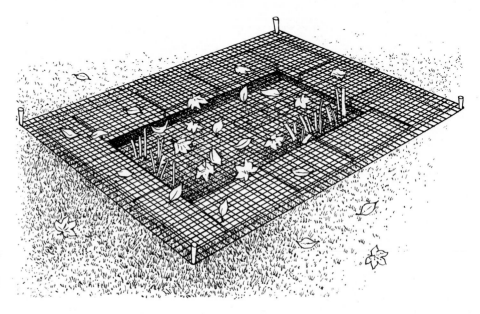

Cover the pool with chicken wire or netting in autumn to catch falling leaves. This prevents them from rotting in the water and producing harmful methane gas

WINTER

In order to release harmful gases, check that thick ice does not remain on the surface for long periods by using a submerged heater or thawing the ice in a small area. Never break ice by heavy blows; these will cause harmful shock waves which may well kill fish and, in any case, the hole will freeze over again in a short time.

When severe weather is forecast, insert floating materials such as logs, which will help to prevent damage by expanding ice. If the severe weather is likely to be prolonged, drop the water level under the ice by an inch or two by syphoning off or baling.

A pool heater is the best means of keeping an ice-free area and costs very little to run

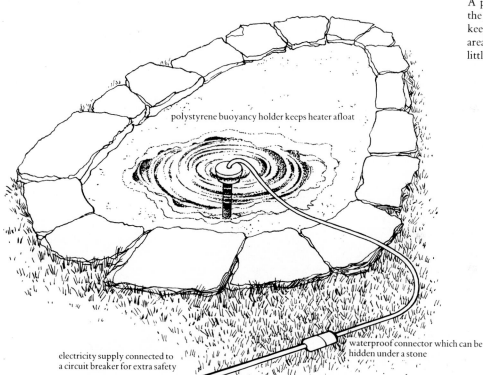

polystyrene buoyancy holder keeps heater afloat

waterproof connector which can be hidden under a stone

electricity supply connected to a circuit breaker for extra safety

The changing face of a pool through the year

Opposite: The pool in early summer

Left: The pool in late summer

Below: The same pool in winter

6
Pests, Diseases and other Troubles

The nature of water gardens, particularly where fish are present, makes chemical control of pests and diseases difficult, if not impossible. In most cases where pest damage is reaching serious proportions, handpicking of infected areas is recommended. Fortunately, the fish themselves control a fair proportion of insect pests by devouring the larvae. In extreme cases where chemicals have to be resorted to, remove the plants from the water, treat them by immersing them in a bucket of dilute pesticide or fungicide, and return to the pool after a thorough rinsing.

PESTS

Waterlily aphis (*Rhopalosiphum nymphaeae*)
Symptoms: Small black aphis covering and disfiguring waterlily leaves and marginals. *Control:* Frequent heavy washing of the foliage. Spray any adjacent cherry trees with a winter ovicide, as these trees act as winter hosts for the eggs.

Waterlily beetle (*Galerucella nymphaeae*)
Symptoms: Small, dark brown beetles the size of a ladybird and black larvae on foliage and flowers of waterlilies, stripping the leaf surface. *Control:* Heavy washing of the foliage and removing remains of poolside plants in the autumn.

China-mark moth (*Nymphula nympheata, N. stagnata*)
Symptoms: Foliage of aquatics being cut and shredded by caterpillars. *Control:* Handpicking or netting the oval pieces of foliage that house the larvae.

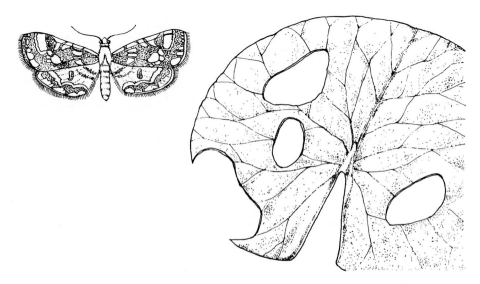

The China-mark moth and an example of the damage its caterpillars can do to a waterlily leaf

False leaf-mining midge (*Cricotopus ornatus*)
Symptoms: Tunnelling marks in the foliage, in severe cases reducing leaves to complete skeletons. *Control:* Remove infected leaves.

DISEASES

Leaf spot (*Ovularia nymphaearum, Cercosporae* spp.)
Symptoms: Dark spots around the edges of waterlily leaves, which later rot and the foliage dies. *Control:* Remove infected plants quickly.

Waterlily root rot (*Pythium* sp.)
Symptoms: Leaf and flower stems soft and blackened, with rotting, smelly, jelly-like areas on roots. *Control:* Remove plants and destroy them.

OTHER DISORDERS

Discoloration in water
If the water is green, check that the surface and submerged planting adequately deprives the offending microscopic algae of mineral salts. As a temporary measure algicides may be used, but the water will probably green up again in time if the planting balance is incorrect. If the water is dark or milky, remove rotting vegetation from the base of the pool.

A to Z of
Pool and Waterside
Plants

Scotney Castle in Kent, an example of water in a romantic setting
(see page 18)

AQUATIC PLANTS

ACORUS Araceae

Striking aquatic perennials with iris-like foliage, aromatic when bruised. The name is derived from the Greek *kore*, a pupil, alluding to the ophthalmic uses of the plant.

A. calamus (sweet flag) Green, iris-like leaves, which give off a strong, tangerine-like scent when crushed. The insignificant, brownish-green flowers are 5–8 cm (2–3 in) long spikes which are densely packed and grow towards the top of the stems. Propagation by division in spring. Height 60–65 cm (2–2½ ft); planting depth 15–30 cm (6–12 in).

A. calamus 'Variegatus' (variegated sweet flag) A variegated form of *A. calamus* with green and creamy white striped, aromatic leaves. The flowers are insignificant, brownish green spikes 5–8 cm (2–3 in) long, which grow close together towards the tops of the stems. This is a very attractive, slower growing, and more compact plant than *A. calamus*. Propagation by division in spring. Height 45–60 cm (1½–2 ft); planting depth 15–30 cm (6–12 in).

A. gramineus (Japanese rush) An attractive dwarf, clump forming, slender-leaved plant, ideal for the small pool or tub garden. The almost grass-like, dark green leaves are evergreen and resemble a dwarf iris. Easily propagated by division in spring. Height 30 cm (12 in); planting depth 5–15 cm (2–6 in).

A. gramineus 'Variegatus' (variegated Japanese rush) A slender-leaved, variegated plant with green and cream stripes running down the leaf. The plant grows in close tufts to about 25 cm (10 in) tall, making it ideally suited to a small pool or tub. The variegation is so attractive that it is grown as a house plant. Propagation by division in spring. Height 30 cm (12 in); planting depth 5–15 cm (2–6 in).

ALISMA Alismataceae

A small group of hardy shallow-water aquatic plants, with plantain-like leaves and small, rosy-coloured flowers borne in whorled panicles throughout the summer.

A. plantago-aquatica (water plantain) The leaves are medium green, slightly heart shaped, with distinct veining and on long stalks. Eye-catching pyramid-shaped flower head about 60 cm (2 ft) high, bearing an abundance of three-petalled, rosy-lilac flowers which open in the afternoon. Remove spent flower heads if seeding becomes a problem. Propagation by seed in spring or by division. Height 60 cm (2 ft); planting depth 5–15 cm (2–6 in).

A. subcordatum This attractive plant bears pyramidal panicles of small pink or white flowers which rise above the rounded foliage. It is quick to establish itself in the pool. During the winter the leaves fall into the water and become skeletonized. Propagation by division of established plants or by seed sown in shallow pans covered by shallow water in spring. Also known as *A. parviflora*. Height 45 cm (1½ ft); planting depth 5–15 cm (2–6 in).

Butomus umbellatus (flowering rush) Butomaceae

A very striking plant, with long, narrow, rich green leaves, triangular in section, tapering to a point at their tips and often reaching 90 cm (3 ft) in height. The flowering stalks are even taller, and are umbels of up to thirty beautiful, dainty pink flowers. A marshland plant. Propagation by division. Height 90–120 cm (3–4 ft); planting depth 8–12 cm (3–5 in).

Calla palustris (bog arum) Araceae
A plant with beautiful dark green, shiny, cordate leaves about 20 cm (8 in) long, borne on a long, creeping rhizome. In early summer the plants are covered with small, arum-like flowers with orange spiky centres. If pollinated by water snails the flowers turn into stout red spikes of striking red berries in the autumn. Propagate by breaking off pieces of rootstock in spring and inserting these into wet soil by the water's edge. Height 23 cm (9 in); planting depth 5–10 cm (2–4 in).

CALTHA Ranunculaceae

A genus of perennial plants thriving equally well in moist soil or shallow water. The name *Caltha*, derived from the Greek *kalathos*, a goblet, refers to the flower shape. Members of the genus should always be grown in clumps for maximum effect.

C. palustris (marsh marigold or king cup) The first aquatic plant to bloom in the spring, with masses of brilliant, golden yellow, buttercup-like flowers. The cordate leaves are dark green and shiny and the whole plant quickly forms bold tufts of dark green with stout, branching stems. Highly recommended as one of the best marginal plants. Propagation is by root division or seed in spring. Height 30 cm (1 ft); planting depth 0–8 cm (0–3 in).

C. palustris 'Alba' An extremely attractive cultivar producing small white flowers with bright yellow stamens in the centre. The leaves are rounded, with a finely serrated edge. A charming addition to every type of pool. Propagation is by root division. Height 15–23 cm (6–9 in); planting depth 0–5 cm (0–2 in).

C. palustris 'Flore Pleno' (double marsh marigold) A really beautiful plant, which produces so many very double flowers that the 23 cm (9 in) high hummock of leaves is almost hidden. It often flowers twice in one year. Propagation by root division. Height 23–30 cm (9–12 in); planting depth 0–5 cm (0–2 in).

C. polypetala (giant marsh marigold) This plant produces an abundance of attractive, large, single yellow flowers rising above large, dark green leaves. A truly magnificent plant for the larger pool. Propagation is by division. Height 90 cm (3 ft); planting depth 0–13 cm (0–5 in).

Cotula coronopifolia (golden buttons or brass buttons) Compositae
A delightful little annual plant with smooth, creeping stems and small leaves that give off a pleasant scent when crushed. It has a very long flowering period, when it is covered with masses of round, golden flowers like buttons. Excellent as an aquatic or marginal plant for all types of pool. Propagation by seed. Height 23 cm (9 in); planting depth 0–10 cm (0–5 in).

CYPERUS Cyperaceae

A large genus of the sedge family, mostly tropical and generally a native of wet areas, grown for their foliage. It has been a genus of great economic importance, providing food, flavourings and fibrous material.

Calla palustris, a yellow-flowered cultivar (see page 81)

C. eragrostis Grass-like leaves growing in tufts, from the centres of which the flower stems are produced, bearing reddish-mahogany umbels. Not as tall as *Cyperus longus*. Propagation by division. Also known as *C. vegetus*. Height 60 cm (2 ft); planting depth 0–10 cm (0–4 in).

C. longus (sweet galingale) A useful plant with smooth, three-sided, leafy green stems bearing reddish-brown,

Caltha palustris and *C. palustris* 'Flore Pleno' (see page 81)

arching, leafy umbels. It is a delight to the flower arranger and is particularly suitable for the larger pool as a good stabilizer of the banks. Propagation by division. Height 90–120 cm (3–4 ft); planting depth 8–12 cm (3–5 in).

Eriophorum angustifolium (cotton grass) Cyperaceae
A tufted plant with slender stems supporting numerous rush-like leaves. The main attraction of the plant is the silky, cottonwool-like seedheads. Propagation is by seed or by division of the rootstock. Height 30–35 cm (12–15 in); planting depth 0–5 cm (0–2 in).

Glyceria aquatica 'Variegata' (sweet grass) Graminae
A beautiful variegated but vigorous grass with stripes of green, yellow and white the length of the leaves. An added attraction is that the young foliage is flushed deep rose in the spring. It is very invasive and in small ponds should be kept in planting crates. Propagate by division. Also known as *G. spectabilis* 'Variegata'. Height 60 cm (2 ft); planting depth 8–12 cm (3–5 in).

HOUTTUYNIA Saururaceae

A genus of hardy aquatic perennials for the waterside. When bruised, the leaves have a strong orange smell. If grown in sunny situations the leaves take on rich autumn tints.

H. cordata A very attractive carpeting plant with bluish-green, heart-shaped leaves on reddish stems, which make an excellent background for the creamy white flowers. In sunny positions the plant will take on rich autumnal colours. This plant is very invasive. Propagation by division.

Eriophorum
angustifolium

Height 15–30 cm (6–12 in); planting depth 5–10 cm (2–4 in).

H. cordata 'Flore Pleno' This delightful double form develops cone-like white flowers. The leaves are heart shaped, bluish-green in colour on reddish stems. If bruised the leaves give off a smell of oranges. Propagation by division. Height 15–30 cm (6–12 in); planting depth 5–10 cm (2–4 in).

IRIS Iridaceae

A large genus, including many plants that thrive in moist soil and several species that are true aquatics, flourishing in water at the pool margin.

I. kaempferi A really beautiful iris from Japan, with large, clematis-like flowers, the horizontal petals looking like large butterflies and covering a wide range of colours. The sword-like green leaves show a prominent midrib. A striking plant for the bog garden, preferring moisture in the summer and drier conditions in the winter. Likes an acid soil. Propagation by division or by seed. This species should now be called *I. ensata* but it is still known as *I. kaempferi* in the trade. Height 45–60 cm (1½–2 ft); planting depth 0–3 cm (0–1 in).

I. kaempferi **Higo strain** A remarkable strain of iris, producing really magnificent clematis-like flowers of enormous size and colour. The flowers can measure as much as 25 cm (10 in) across. These irises prefer moisture in the summer and drier conditions in the winter. Remarkably resistant to strong wind. Propagation by division in spring. Height 45–60 cm ($1\frac{1}{2}$–2 ft); planting depth 0–3 cm (0–1 in).

I. kaempferi 'Variegata' This plant has everything, from large, beautiful clematis-like flowers in a wide range of colours to delightfully variegated leaves showing cream and green stripes along their length. Propagation by division in spring. Height 60 cm (2 ft); planting depth 0–3 cm (0–1 in).

I. laevigata This is really one of the finest aquatics for early summer. The flowers are blue, with golden-yellow markings on the fall petals, and are 10–15 cm (4–6 in) across. The smooth, light green leaves grow 60 cm (2 ft) tall. This plant is very suitable for a small pool. Propagation by division in spring. Height 30–60 cm (1–2 ft); planting depth 5–7 cm (2–3 in).

I. laevigata 'Atropurpurea' A very striking cultivar of *Iris laevigata*, with its beautiful flowers almost a violet colour and showing up extremely well against the elegant, sword-like leaves. This plant is extremely suitable for the small pool. Propagation by division in spring. Height 60–75 cm (2–$2\frac{1}{2}$ ft); planting depth 8–10 cm (3–5 in)

I. laevigata 'Colchesteri' This beautiful cultivar has large white flowers which are heavily mottled with dark blue on the edges of the fall petals. It is very suitable for small pools. Propagation by division in spring. Height 75 cm ($2\frac{1}{2}$ ft); planting depth 8–12 cm (3–5 in).

I. laevigata 'Monstrosa' This cultivar has huge violet and white flowers. Height 90 cm (2 ft); planting depth 5–10 cm (2–4 in).

I. laevigata 'Mottled Beauty' A mottled form of *Iris laevigata*, the attractive blue markings showing up well against the creamy-white colour of the petals, becoming more pronounced as the plant matures. Propagation by division in spring. Height 60 cm (2 ft); planting depth 5–10 cm (2–4 in).

I. laevigata 'Rose Queen' This cultivar is possibly a hybrid with *Iris kaempferi* and is unique in having large, soft, rose-pink flowers and graceful, grass-like foliage. It is at home in the water or in the surrounding damp soil. A very useful addition to any pool. Propagation by division in spring. Height 60 cm (2 ft); planting depth 0–2.5 cm (0–1 in).

I. laevigata 'Snowdrift' An exceptionally large and beautiful iris, bearing snow-white flowers with a pale yellow base to the petals. Suitable for all types of pool, but especially good in the smaller ones. Propagation by division in spring. Height 75 cm ($2\frac{1}{2}$ ft); planting depth 5–10 cm (2–4 in).

I. laevigata 'Variegata' An exceptionally attractive addition to any pool. As well as producing lavender blue flowers, it has leaves with well defined variegations in green and cream running lengthways, and the whole plant grows in a distinctive fan shape. Propagation by division in spring. Height 60 cm (2 ft); planting depth 0–8 cm (0–3 in).

I. pseudacorus (yellow flag iris) A very vigorous plant, producing rich yellow flowers on tall stems. The sword-like leaves grow to 90 cm (3 ft). This plant is not suitable for small pools, but looks superb at the edge of large areas of water. Propagation by division in early autumn or spring. Height 90 cm (3 ft); planting depth 0–15 cm (0–6 in).

I. pseudacorus 'Bastardi' Flowers soft primrose yellow and very free flowering, just as vigorous as the type, but will grow in marshy ground or shallow water. Height 60–75 cm (2–2½ ft); planting depth 8–13 cm (3–5 in).

I. pseudacorus 'Golden Queen'
This form of the native *Iris pseudacorus* is a slightly more refined cultivar, and bears large, vivid yellow flowers and a slightly wider leaf. Not really suitable for small pools. Propagation by division in spring. Height 90 cm (3 ft); planting depth 8–13 cm (3–5 in).

I. pseudacorus 'Sulphur Queen' Another plant better suited to the larger pool. The large flowers are paler and more primrose yellow than the native yellow flag iris. The sword-like leaves reach about 90 cm (3 ft) in height. Propagation by division in spring. Height 90 cm (3 ft); planting depth 8–13 cm (3–5 in).

I. pseudacorus 'Variegata' A fine form of *I. pseudacorus*, with very attractive leaf variegations in gold and green that fade rapidly towards the end of summer. This plant also produces bright golden-yellow flowers. Propagation by division in spring. Height 45–60 cm (1½–2 ft); planting depth 5–10 cm (2–4 in).

I. versicolor A plant native to North America that produces very attractive and finely shaped violet-blue flowers with conspicuous yellow patches at the base of the petals. The leaves are sword-like and grow to about 60 cm (2 ft) in height. Propagation by division in spring or by seed in autumn. Height 45–60 cm (1½–2 ft); planting depth 5–10 cm (2–4 in).

I. versicolor 'Kermesina' A really beautiful cultivar, bearing vivid claret-magenta flowers marked with white. Suitable for small pools. Propagation by division in spring. Height 45–60 cm (1½–2 ft); planting depth 5–10 cm (2–4 in).

Juncus effusus var. spiralis (corkscrew rush) Juncaceae
An interesting plant grown purely for its tall, green, cylindrical stems which grow twisted in a corkscrew fashion. A talking point in any pool, and much sought after by the flower arranger. Propagation by division. Height 45 cm (1½ ft); planting depth 8–13 cm (3–5 in).

Lobelia cardinalis (cardinal flower) Campanulaceae
This eye-catching plant, with its tapering spikes of vivid scarlet flowers and green foliage, is usually thought of as a border plant needing some protection. In fact in water 8–10 cm (3–4 in) deep it is quite hardy and makes a striking waterside plant, especially where the reflection can be seen. Propagation by division, seed or cuttings. Some hybrids of *L. cardinalis* have reddish foliage. Height 90 cm (3 ft); planting depth 5–8 cm (2–3 in).

LYSICHITUM Araceae

A genus of two hardy, vigorous plants belonging to the same family as the native arum, having large ornamental spathes and spadices. The name is derived from the Greek *lysis*, loose and *chiton*, cloak, referring to the spathe, which is shed as the flowers age.

L. americanum A very handsome North American plant. The large, 30 cm (1 ft) high, deep yellow spathes of the arum-like flowers have a thick,

Opposite:
Myosotis scorpioides
(see page 88)

Right: *Menyanthes trifoliata*

parchment-like texture. They appear in the early spring before the large green leaves. This plant has considerable architectural merit. Propagation by division, seed and self-set seedlings. Height 60 cm (2 ft); planting depth 0–2.5 cm (0–1 in).

L. camtschatcense This plant from Japan has very attractive, pure white spathes which are almost translucent,

Mimulus luteus

and are like the arum lily in shape. The leaves are large, green and pointed. An easily grown plant in either shallow water or wet soil, and certainly one to be recommended for any pool. Propagation by division and by self-set seedlings. Height 30 cm (1 ft); planting depth 0–2.5 cm (0–1 in).

Mentha aquatica (water mint) Labiatae
A vigorous plant with strongly aromatic, oval hairy, toothed leaves, which are almost obscured in late summer by clustered spikes of pale lavender flowers that are very attractive to bees. Propagation by division. Height 23–30 cm (9–12 in); planting depth 0–8 cm (0–3 in).

Menyanthes trifoliata (bog bean) Menyanthaceae
An extremely useful plant for hiding the edges of artificial pools because of its scrambling habit. The leaves are like those of the broad bean and grow in threes on a single stem. They are one of the food plants of the elephant hawk moth larvae. In early spring the flowers appear on spikes; they are pink in the bud but open to reveal fringed white petals. Propagation by division. Height 23–30 cm (9–12 in); planting depth 5–10 cm (2–4 in).

MIMULUS Scrophulariaceae

A genus of hardy annual, half-hardy perennial, and hardy perennial plants grown for their showy flowers, which provide a riot of colour throughout the summer.

M. luteus (monkey musk) This attractive plant produces throughout the summer an abundance of bright yellow flowers speckled with red. The leaf edges are serrated, a light green in colour and smooth surfaced. The plant makes quite an impact when planted

in clumps in shallow water. Propagation by division, seed or cuttings. Height 30 cm (1 ft); planting depth 0–5 cm (0–2 in).

M. luteus 'A.T. Johnston' This cultivar bears rich yellow flowers mottled with maroon from June to September. Height 25–30 cm (9–12 in); planting depth 0–5 cm (0–2 in).

M. ringens (lavender musk) A truly aquatic musk which will also grow in shallow water. It has tall, erect, square, much branched stems carrying narrow, oblong leaves and delicate blue or bluish-violet flowers in summer. An attractive addition to any pool. Propagation by division, seed or cuttings. Height 45 cm (18 in); planting depth 7–12 cm (3–5 in).

Myosotis scorpioides (water forget-me-not) Boraginaceae
An ideal native plant for the pool edge, with its oblong, hairy leaves, and bright blue flowers with yellow or pink eyes. It seeds well and thrives even in shade. An excellent choice. Propagation by seed. Also known as *M. palustris*. Height 23–30 cm (9–12 in); planting depth 0–8 cm (0–3 in).

Myriophyllum aquaticum (parrot's feather) Haloragaceae
An attractive and doubly useful plant, because the underwater growth will act as an oxygenator while the foliage above the water surface trails attractively. It is feathery, with finely cut, light green leaves, which grow in dense clusters around the stems with upturned tips. In late summer these tips turn crimson and can be destroyed by frost. Propagation by cuttings of overwintered plants. Also called *M. proserpinacoides*. Height 15–20 cm (6–8 in); planting depth 8–15 cm (3–6 in).

NYMPHAEA (waterlily)
Nymphaeaceae

There are both hardy and tropical species of waterlily, the most important plants of all. The selection given here is shown under flower colour and planting depth in the chart on page 116–17.

SPECIES

N. alba This species, which is distributed over a wide area of Europe, including Britain, and Asia, is mainly found in large lakes or slow-moving rivers. It is a robust and hardy species, not really suitable for domestic ponds. The cup-shaped flowers are snowy white, containing yellow stamens and surrounded by large cordate foliage which hugs the water. Approx. spread 2.5 m (8 ft). Adaptable to water 38–90 cm (15–36 in) deep.

N. candida A species with a wide distribution, ranging across northern Europe, Asia, and south to the Himalayas. It is a very tough and hardy species, making it a good choice for colder areas. The white flowers are cup shaped, containing red stigmas, and are held high above the water. The light green foliage has prominent veins on the undersides. Approx. spread 60 cm (2 ft). Adaptable to water 15–30 cm (6–12 in) deep.

N. odorata var. alba This pure white, fragrant North American waterlily has cup-shaped and prolific flowers that are surface floating, surrounded by pale green leaves that are purple when young. It prefers shallow water, but with room to spread. Approx. spread 1.5 m (5 ft). Adaptable to water 23–60 cm (9–24 in) deep.

N. odorata var. minor A dwarf white waterlily which is found in shallow swamps in North America. It can be successfully grown in tubs or shallow pools, but requires full sun. The small, star-shaped, sweetly scented flowers have brown stems and are freely produced. The foliage is light green with dark red undersides. Approx. spread 60 cm (2 ft). Adaptable to water 15–30 cm (6–12 in) deep.

N. odorata var. rosea The Cape Cod waterlily, which bears medium sized, fragrant flowers of a soft pink which deepen in colour towards the centre. It is at home in the margins of very large pools where it has room to develop in the shallow regions. This desire for space makes it more of a collector's item than an ideal variety for the small to medium pool. It is interesting historically because of its discovery in America as ground tubers in a low-lying valley on ground that had been recently ploughed. When it was found that these tubers were beautiful pink waterlilies, they were introduced into cultivation and were the source of the present commercial stocks. All the American N. odorata hybrids have proved to be capable of survival in dried-up ponds. Approx. spread 1.5 m (5 ft). Adaptable to water 23–60 cm (9–24 in) deep.

N. pygmaea 'Alba' This native of China and Japan is one of the smallest of the white varieties, and is suitable for tubs, sinks and shallow pools. The small, star-like flowers contain bright golden stamens. The profuse foliage is small, light green and rounded. Approx. spread 40 cm (16 in). Adaptable to water 38–90 cm (15–36 in) deep.

N. pygmaea 'Rubra' This may be a difficult plant to find commercially. It is a true miniature suitable for very small bowls and tubs. The flowers

open dark pink, the outer petals being white blushed with pink that age to a rich maroon red. The foliage is green with a reddish undersurface. Approx. spread 40 cm (16 in). Adaptable to water 15–23 cm (6–9 in) deep.

N. tuberosa var. rosea An exceptionally strong-growing variety, which has very fragrant, medium sized flowers which are soft pink, shaded white, and carried along the surface. Bright red stamens. The abundant pale green leaves are demanding in space, requiring fairly deep water. Approx. spread 2.5 m (8 ft). Adaptable to water 38–90 cm (15–36 in) deep.

N. tuberosa 'Richardsonii' A robust and vigorous white cultivar, one of the first to flower and continuing until late September. The large globular flowers have distinctive pea-green sepals and golden yellow stamens. It is only truly at home in lakes or natural ponds. Approx. spread 2.5 m (8 ft). Adaptable to water 38–90 cm (15–36 in) deep.

HYBRIDS

×**laydekeri 'Fulgens'** One of the most vivid of red-flowered waterlilies, with fiery red stamens and attractive green sepals which are rose-coloured inside. Fragrant. Approx. spread 90 cm (3 ft). Adaptable to water 15–23 cm (6–9 in) deep.

×**laydekeri 'Lilacea'** A free-flowering plant with fragrant, cup-shaped flowers which open a soft rose and white colour, deepening to rose and crimson. The dark green sepals, are edged with rose and the stamens are bright yellow. There are very slight markings on the leaves. It is a very popular plant for tub cultivation. Approx. spread 60 cm (2 ft). Adaptable to water 15–30 cm (6–12 in) deep.

Nymphaea
×marliacea
'Chromatella'

×*laydekeri* **'Purpurata'** The flowers are a crimson red and prolifically produced for the whole season, with strongly pointed petals carrying bright orange stamens. The leaves bear maroon markings on the surface, and are purplish underneath. Approx. spread 60–90 cm (2–3 ft). Adaptable to water 15–23 cm (6–9 in) deep.

×*marliacea* **'Albida'** A remarkably free flowering, fragrant, white-flowered hybrid, which carries the flowers above the water surface. The conspicuous bronze green sepals contain golden stamens. The large, deep green leaves have purple undersides and are vigorous spreaders. Approx. spread 2 m (6 ft). Adaptable to water 23–60 cm (9–24 in) deep.

×*marliacea* **'Carnea'** In the first year after planting the flowers are almost white, and though they develop a pink flush with age from a distance they could be thought to be a white hybrid. It is exceptionally vigorous and free flowering, and is one of the most commonly cultivated waterlilies. Strong vanilla-like scent. The large leaves turn from purple to deep green with age. It is sometimes listed as 'Morning Glory'. Approx. spread 2 m

Nymphaea
'Escarboucle' (see
page 92)

(6 ft). Adaptable to water 30–75 cm (12–30 in) deep.

×*marliacea* **'Chromatella'** Very free-flowering, the large, soft yellow flowers stay open later in the day than most other hybrids. It has attractive dark green foliage, conspicuously mottled and spotted reddish-brown. It is sometimes called 'Golden Cup'. Approx. spread 2 m (6 ft). Adaptable to water 30–75 cm (12–30 in) deep.

×*marliacea* **'Rosea'** As with ×*marliacea* 'Carnea', this beautiful hybrid (the first of the Marliac hybrids) may be disappointing initially, as it has a tendency to develop its true shade of glowing rose colour in later years. It could easily be confused with 'Carnea', but has a deeper flush of rose. Extremely fragrant. The foliage turns from purple to dark green with age. Approx. spread 2 m (6 ft). Adaptable to water 30–75 cm (12–30 in) deep.

CULTIVARS — MOSTLY OF HYBRID ORIGIN

'Albatross' The large, star-shaped and snow-white flowers, with distinctive narrow petals, contain a cluster of golden stamens. The purplish leaves change to dark green with age.

Nymphaea 'James Brydon' (see page 93)

Approx. spread 120 cm (4 ft). Adaptable to water 23–45 cm (9–18 in) deep.

'Amabilis' Very beautiful with large, flat, star-shaped flowers of light pink to salmon colour. The fine stamens are yellow, intensifying to fiery orange and darkening with age as the foliage also changes, from dark red to olive green. It is sometimes called 'Pink Marvel'. Approx. spread 2 m (6 ft). Adaptable to water 30–75 cm (12–30 in) deep.

'Atropurpurea' A very intense shade of crimson red petals surrounding conspicuous yellow stamens. The young leaves are dark red, turning to a dark green with age. Approx. spread 1.5 m (5 ft). Adaptable to water 23–60 cm (9–24 in) deep.

'Attraction' Closely resembling the better known 'Atropurpurea', its glowing shade of garnet red petals, slightly flaked with white and containing rich mahogany stamens, makes it an attractive cultivar for large pools, where it needs all the space it can get. Approx. spread 2.5 m (8 ft). Adaptable to water 38–90 cm (15–36 in) deep.

'Aurora' The name of this plant gives a clue to its attraction of changing flower colours, ranging from coppery yellow to salmon-orange and later a rich ruby red. As with many of the yellow hybrids, the leaves are mottled and marbled. It is particularly suitable for shallow water. Approx. spread 60 cm (2 ft). Adaptable to water 23–60 m (9–24 in) deep.

'Charles de Meurville' This extremely vigorous cultivar is one of the first to flower, producing its plum-coloured, 25 cm (10 in) blooms from early May. Its huge leaves are nearly 45 cm (18 in) across and a handsome olive colour. Approx. spread 2.5 m (8 ft). Adaptable to water 38–90 cm (15–36 in) deep.

'Colonel A. J. Welch' One of the most vigorous waterlilies in cultivation, this cultivar could only be recommended for very expansive situations where a yellow flower is specified. The canary yellow flowers, raised just above the water surface, are sparsely produced in relation to the masses of faintly mottled leaves. Approx. spread 2.5 m (8 ft). Adaptable to water 38–75 cm (15–36 in) deep.

'Colossea' An exceptionally vigorous hybrid, producing its huge flesh-pink flowers from May to October. The fragrant blooms turn white with age, surrounded by the dark olive green leaves. Approx. spread 2.5 m (8 ft). Adaptable to water 38–90 cm (15–36 in) deep.

'Comanche' The flowers, which change from apricot-yellow to a rich copper-red with yellow outer petals, are held well above the water surface. These colours are enhanced by deep orange-red stamens, and young foliage which turns from purple to green with age. Approx. spread 90 cm (3 ft). Adaptable to water 18–38 cm (7–15 in) deep.

'Conqueror' An extremely attractive, free-flowering cultivar with large, cup-shaped, crimson, incurving petals with contrasting white sepals. The young foliage is purple and compact in growth, changing to green with age. Approx. spread 2 m (6 ft). Adaptable to water 23–60 cm (9–24 in) deep.

'Ellisiana' A must for tubs or small pools where small, deep red flowers are required. It is easy to grow and reliable in its flowering, which is enhanced by attractive orange-red stamens emerging from the purple bases to the petals. Approx. spread 60 cm (2 ft). Adaptable to water 15–23 cm (6–9 in) deep.

'Escarboucle' One of the most outstanding cultivars of waterlily because of its colour, reliability and vigour. The large blooms, of intense vermilion crimson, are produced in quantity, some reaching nearly 30 cm (1 ft) across. The fragrant crimson petals contrast perfectly with the rich yellow anthers to the reddish filaments. It is also called 'Aflame'. Approx. spread 2 m (6 ft). Adaptable to water 23–60 cm (9–24 in) deep.

'Froebeli' The fragrant, blood-red flowers and orange stamens make this classic colour combination a most popular choice; in addition it offers reliability and a free-flowering habit. Approx. spread 90 cm (3 ft). Adaptable to water 15–23 cm (6–9 in) deep.

'Gladstoniana' One of the most beautiful white hybrids, with exceptionally large, fragrant blooms up to 25 cm (10 in) across, full of golden stamens and surrounded by sepals with touches of green. The large leaves tend to push out of the water, which is remedied by planting in a minimum depth of 60 cm (2 ft). Approx. spread 2.5 m (8 ft). Adaptable to water 38–90 cm (15–36 in) deep.

'Gloire de Temple-sur-Lot' This fine plant is quite distinct from any other hybrid, with its full double flowers containing up to a hundred finely cut, incurving petal segments. The young flower, containing bright yellow stamens, is rose pink, changing to white with age. It is unfortunately not very prolific in flowering. Approx. spread 2 m (6 ft). Adaptable to water 23–60 cm (9–24 in) deep.

'Gloriosa' The ability to tolerate light shade gives an additional bonus to this hybrid, with its bright red, fragrant blooms which are semi-double containing reddish orange stamens. It is a firm favourite in America and should prove more popular in Europe. Approx. spread 120 cm (4 ft). Adaptable to water 23–45 cm (9–18 in) deep.

'Gonnère' A very good double cultivar, with paeony-shaped, snow-white flowers with thick petals and outer green sepals. The flowers, which remain in good condition for a long period, contain a bright display of golden yellow anthers, surrounded by green leaves of modest spread. It is also known as 'Crystal White'. Approx. spread 1.5 m (5 ft). Adaptable to water 23–60 cm (9–24 in) deep.

'Graziella' The small flowers have an unusual shade of reddish copper passing to orange-yellow, enhanced by bright orange stamens. The light green foliage has handsome purple mottling. It is a very good cultivar for tubs. Approx. spread 90 cm (3 ft). Adaptable to water 18–38 cm (7–15 in) deep.

'Hal Miller' This vigorous hybrid, which is a relatively recent introduction, has rich creamy flowers held well above the water surface. Approx. spread 1.5 m (5 ft). Adaptable to water 23–60 cm (9–24 in) deep.

'Helen Fowler' The large flowers are an exquisite shade of rich pink, are fragrant, and are held well above the water. This *odorata* hybrid is becoming increasingly difficult to obtain. The leaves are a soft green and not too demanding in space – it is suitable for tubs or small pools. Approx. spread 120 cm (4 ft). Adaptable to water 23–45 cm (9–18 in) deep.

'Helvola' The ideal hybrid for growing in a tub or small pool, with its dainty, star-shaped, canary yellow flowers which are produced in abundance throughout the summer. The tiny olive-green leaves are mottled with purple and brown markings. Approx. spread 40 cm (16 in). Adaptable to water 15–23 cm (6–9 in) deep.

'Hermine' The pure white flowers stand well above the water on stiff stems and are produced profusely over a long period. The outer sepals are stained green and the medium sized, oval foliage is a dark green. Approx. spread 90 cm (3 ft). Adaptable to water 18–30 cm (7–12 in) deep.

'Indiana' An outstanding free-flowering cultivar with the flowers changing from rich orange-red to brilliant copper-red as they age. The leaves are heavily mottled with purple. Approx. spread 120 cm (4 ft). Adaptable to water 23–45 cm (9–18 in) deep.

'James Brydon' Deservedly one of the most popular of all waterlilies, which in addition to its many aesthetic attributes will tolerate a degree of shade. Its freely produced, fragrant, cup-like flowers are a rich carmine-red colour, with orange stamens tipped with yellow. These flowers are perfectly complemented by the circular, bronze to dark green foliage. It will tolerate a wide range of water depths, from tubs to natural and extensive pools. Approx. spread 120 cm (4 ft). Adaptable to water 23–45 cm (9–18 in) deep.

Nymphaea 'Rose Arey' (see page 96)

'Masaniello' The fragrant, rose-pink, paeony-shaped flowers are exceptionally large and held above the water surface. Their pink colour intensifies to a deep carmine with age. Sepals white with orange stamens. Approx. spread 1.5 m (5 ft). Adaptable to water 23–60 cm (9–24 in) deep.

'Mme. Wilfron Gonnère' This outstanding cultivar is one of few bearing double flowers. They are soft pink, flushed with white, with a deeper shade of pink nearer the centre. The leaves are plain green. Approx. spread 1.5 m (5 ft). Adaptable to water 23–60 cm (9–24 in) deep.

'Moorei' One of the brightest and most highly coloured of the yellow hybrids, with primrose-yellow blooms. The pale green leaves are irregularly sprinkled with brown spots. Approx. spread 1.5 m (5 ft). Adaptable to water 23–60 cm (9–24 in) deep.

'Mrs Richmond' The very large globular flowers, prolifically produced, are a pale rose pink on opening,

'Loose' A fragrant American cultivar with pure white, star-like flowers that are held on stout stems almost 30 cm (1 ft) above the water. Approx. spread 120 cm (4 ft). Adaptable to water 23–45 cm (9–18) deep.

'Lucida' The pale pink, star-shaped flowers, containing orange stamens, change with age to a beautiful rose-vermilion colour. The leaves are an attractive feature of this cultivar, having an almost purple marbling on the surface. Approx. spread 120 cm (4 ft). Adaptable to water 23–45 cm (9–18 in) deep.

'Lustrous' The prolific and beautiful flowers have broad, soft pink petals with a velvety texture, containing the yellow stamens. The sepals have a pink interior with brown undersides. The young leaves are a copper colour, turning to dark green with age. Approx. spread 120 cm (4 ft) Adaptable to water 23–45 cm (9–18 in) deep.

'Mary Patricia' A cultivar which is suitable for small ponds or tub cultivation. It produces most attractive, cup-shaped pink and peach-blossom flowers with great freedom. Approx. spread 90 cm (3 ft). Adaptable to water 20–40 cm (8–16 in) deep.

Nymphaea 'Mme. Wilfron Gonnère'

Nymphaea
'Hermine' (see
page 93)

deepening with age to a deep pink. The petal bases are red, containing very conspicuous golden stamens supported by white sepals. The foliage is a very attractive light green. Approx. spread 2.5 m (8 ft). Adaptable to water 38–90 cm (15–36 in) deep.

'Newton' The brilliant vermilion flowers, with unusually long stamens, stand well above the water giving a star-like appearance with their long, pointed petals. Approx. spread 1.5 m (5 ft). Adaptable to water 23–60 cm (9–24 in) deep.

'Odalisque' A very beautiful cultivar with prolific, soft pink, star-like blooms that change to rose with age.

These blooms, with their bright golden stamens, reflexed sepals, and outer petals are held above the water. Approx. spread 120 cm (4 ft). Adaptable to water 23–45 cm (9–18 in) deep.

'Paul Hariot' A very pretty, free-flowering cultivar which changes colour from apricot-flushed rose to a copper red. The foliage is green, attractively spotted with maroon. Approx. spread 60 cm (2 ft). Adaptable to water 13–30 cm (5–12 in) deep.

'Pink Opal' An interesting and attractive plant which produces flowers nearly 23 cm (9 in) above the water surface that can be used for cutting. These flowers, which in bud are unusually spherical, are a most pleasant coral-pink colour. It makes an ideal subject for tubs, and despite its delicate appearance is easily grown. Approx. spread 90 cm (3 ft). Adaptable to water 20–40 cm (8–16 in) deep.

'Pink Sensation' An unusual feature of this plant is the ability of its flowers to remain open for several hours longer in the evening than those of any other cultivar. The flowers are fragrant, rich pink, with long oval petals held above the water surface. The deep green leaves have reddish undersides. Approx. spread 1.5 m (5 ft). Adaptable to water 23–60 cm (9–24 in) deep.

'René Gérard' The large, rose pink, star-shaped flowers have their stout oval petals blotched and striped with deep crimson near the centre. The leaves are plain green. Approx. spread 1.5 m (5 ft). Adaptable to water 23–60 cm (9–24 in) deep.

'Rose Arey' Large, stellate, rose-pink flowers with fragrant incurving petals and brilliant orange stamens tipped with yellow. The very attractive, rich purple foliage changes to green with age. It is one of the best rose-pink cultivars. Approx. spread 120 cm (4 ft). Adaptable to water 23–45 cm (9–18 in) deep.

'Somptuosa' Deliciously scented, exceptionally large, globular flowers containing vivid orange stamens which contrast well with the rose-pink, velvety petals. It has very compact growth. Approx. spread 90 cm (3 ft). Adaptable to water 20–40 cm (8–16 in) deep.

'Sulphurea Grandiflora' A shy-blooming hybrid, which must be planted in fairly shallow water in warm, sunny conditions. The stellate, multi-petalled flowers are sulphur-yellow in colour and stand well above the water. The leaves are marbled above with chocolate-coloured markings, and spotted with red underneath. Approx. spread 120 cm (4 ft). Adaptable to water 23–45 cm (9–18 in) deep.

'Sunrise' Undoubtedly bearing the largest and most richly coloured flowers of all the yellow waterlilies, 'Sunrise' requires as much warmth and sunshine as possible to flower well in temperate conditions. The huge, fragrant, golden blooms, nearly 25 cm (10 in) across, enhanced by their golden yellow stamens and narrow curving petals, stand well above the water surface. The leaves, with their undulating margins, are green, occasionally blotched with brown, and have reddish undersides. Approx. spread 1.5 m (5 ft). Adaptable to water 23–60 cm (9–24 in) deep.

'Virginalis' An excellent cultivar with beautiful, large white, semi-double flowers containing broad, shell-shaped petals, and snow-white sepals that are rose-tinged towards their bases. This has one of the longest flowering seasons, although it is rather slow to become established. The foliage is green with a purple flush. Approx. spread 2 m (6 ft). Adaptable to water 23–60 cm (9–24 in) deep.

'William Falconer' Similar to 'Atropurpurea' but with more cup-like rather than saucer-shaped flowers. The foliage is dark purple with red veining, changing with age to green. The flowers are very dark red, bearing yellow stamens. Approx. spread 1.5 m (5 ft). Adaptable to water 23–60 cm (9–24 in) deep.

Pontederia cordata (pickerel weed)
Pontederiaceae

Perhaps one of the easiest marginal aquatics for any type of pool, with its neat growth of superb, glossy, heart-shaped leaves growing on smooth, rounded stems. The soft blue flowers grow as spikes, and are produced from summer through to autumn, making it an invaluable addition to any collection. Propagation by division. Height 60 cm (2 ft); planting depth 8–13 cm (3–5 in).

RANUNCULUS Ranunculaceae

Moist ground is the usual habitat of most buttercups, which are widespread, many with an invasive tendency. There are a few suitable for bog gardens in sun or partial shade.

R. flammula (lesser spearwort) A smaller plant than *Ranunculus lingua* 'Grandiflora', and attractive for the smaller pool. The flowers are not so large and have pale yellow, glossy petals. Propagation by division. Height 30 cm (1 ft); planting depth 0–8 cm (0–3 in).

R. lingua **'Grandiflora'** (greater spearwort) A good plant for the larger pool. It grows to about 90 cm (3 ft) in height with thick, deep pink stems and narrow leaves. The flowers are a glistening golden colour, similar to those of the buttercup but much larger. Propagation by division. Height 60–90 cm (2–3 ft); planting depth 8–15 cm (3–6 in).

SAGITTARIA Alismataceae

A genus of about twenty species of aquatic or moisture-loving perennials, at their best in shallow water. They have excellent oxygenating properties.

S. sagittifolia (arrowhead) A plant with beautiful, acutely arrow-shaped leaves, and very attractive spikes of white flowers with black and crimson centres. Suitable for all types of pool. Propagation by division. Height 30–45 cm (1–1½ ft); planting depth 8–13 cm (3–5 in).

S. sagittifolia **'Flore Pleno'** An extremely attractive cultivar of *Sagittaria*. Not only does it have the thrusting arrow-shaped leaves, but the stems on which the double snow-white flowers grow are nearly obscured by the fullness of the petals. Propagation by division. Height 38–45 cm (15–18 in); planting depth 8–15 cm (3–6 in).

Saururus cernuus (swamp lily, lizard's tail) Saururaceae

A useful plant, as not only does it bear heart-shaped leaves and long nodding spikes of fragrant white flowers up to 15 cm (6 in) long in summer, but in autumn the leaves take on rich autumnal tints. Propagation by division. Height 60 cm (2 ft); water depth 0–5 cm (0–2 in).

SCIRPUS Cyperaceae

A cosmopolitan genus containing some 250 species, few of which are grown in garden conditions because of their invasive, stoloniferous habit.

S. lacustris **subsp.** *tabernaemontani* **'Albescens'** A tall plant with round, rushy stems vertically lined with green and cream. Best grown in a container to prevent excessive spreading. Propagation by division. Height 90–120 cm (3–4 ft); planting depth 8–13 cm (3–5 in).

S. lacustris **subsp.** *tabernaemontani* **'Zebrinus'** (zebra rush) A striking foliage plant with its fine horizontally banded stems in green and white. A very distinctive addition to the pool. Propagation by division. Height 30–90 cm (1–3 ft); planting depth 8–13 cm (3–5 in).

Sparganium erectum (bur-reed)
Sparganiaceae

One of the larger aquatic plants, with attractive leaves which are triangular at the base, terminating in a sharp point. The branched inflorescence produces round flowerheads and spiky fruits. This plant is best grown in a container as it is inclined to be rampant. Propagation by division. Also known as *S. ramosum*. Height 75–120 cm (2½–4 ft); planting depth 8–13 cm (3–5 in).

TYPHA Typhaceae

Opposite:
Aponogeton distachyos (see page 101)

Below: *Typha minima*

Handsome plants with long, sword-like leaves of varying widths, and long, poker-like heads of flowers made up of masses of closely packed, chocolate-coloured female flowers with a mass of male flowers above it. They are generally spreaders and need to be controlled.

T. angustifolia (lesser reedmace) A rather stately plant, with graceful grey-green leaves and chocolate-brown, poker-like fruiting heads. It is advisable to grow it in a container as it is rather invasive. It is only suitable for large pools. Propagation by division. Height to 2 m (6 ft); planting depth 0–15 cm (0–6 in).

T. latifolia (great reedmace) This is the giant of the family and is out of scale except in really large water gardens. It produces large, flat, grass-like leaves of a grey-green colour, and thick poker-like heads of flowers. Propagation by division. Height 2–2.5 m (6–8 ft); planting depth 8–13 cm (3–5 in).

T. minima (miniature reedmace) A really delightful dwarf Japanese species with delicate, reed-like leaves bluish green in colour. The pokers are short and chunky and extremely attractive. It is really the only suitable reedmace for small to medium pools. Propagation by division. Height 30–60 cm (1–2 ft); planting depth 0–10 cm (0–4 in).

T. stenophylla (small reedmace) A very much more restrained species producing slender, willowy leaves and attractive dark brown pokers. Propagation by division. Height 90 cm (3 ft); planting depth 0–15 cm (0–6 in).

Veronica beccabunga (brooklime)
Scrophulariaceae

An excellent plant for the pool edge because of its sprawling habit. The creeping stems bear dark green leaves

and floating. It grows in dense, spreading masses which in spring are covered with myriads of five-petalled, snow-white, yellow-centred flowers. Propagation by cuttings.

OTHER SUBMERGED AQUATIC PLANTS

Aponogeton distachyos (water hawthorn) Aponogetonaceae

A most desirable plant for all pools. The beautiful, heavily scented flowers are curiously lobed and forked, and are white in colour with black anthers. They are produced freely in early summer and autumn, and even, weather permitting, sporadically throughout the rest of the year. At planting, submerge no deeper than 15 cm (6 in), then later move into deeper water as required. Floating leaves; planting depth 15–45 cm (6–18 in).

Hottonia palustris (water violet) Primulaceae

A charming floating aquatic plant, particularly for shallow pools. It bears whorls of pale green, much divided leaves with long white roots trailing from the leaf joints. The delicate, lilac-coloured flowers are held well above the water on slender stems. Winter buds are formed in autumn and the plant then disappears until the spring. Propagation by seed or division in May. Height above the water 15–30 cm (6–12 in).

NUPHAR Nymphaeaceae

Nuphars will tolerate very cold conditions, as they are very robust and frost hardy. They will grow in deep water, in shaded positions, sluggish streams and in most places where waterlilies normally fail.

N. lutea (common yellow waterlily)

This has large leaves up to 40 cm (16 in) long and 30 cm (1 ft) wide, with bright yellow flowers. Floating leaves; planting depth 1–2 m (3–6 ft).

N. advena

Originates from the eastern states of North America and one of the best species. It bears rich yellow, globular flowers 5 cm (2 in) in diameter which are tinged with green and purple. There is a cultivar, 'Variegata', available with cream flowers and variegated foliage. Floating leaves; planting depth 1–2 m (3–6 ft).

N. japonica

A Japanese species with yellow flowers 5–7.5 cm (2–3 in) across, and attractive, long, arrow-shaped floating leaves. *N. japonica* var. *rubrotinctum* has orange-red flowers. Floating leaves; planting depth 1–2 m (3–6 ft).

Nymphoides peltatum var. *bennettii* (floating heart) Menyanthaceae

A small floating plant resembling a miniature waterlily, with rounded, bright green leaves and dainty yellow flowers that are held clear of the surface. An ideal plant to give surface cover while waterlilies are becoming established. It is not entirely hardy. Also known as *Limnanthemum nymphoides* var. *bennettii* and *Villarsia bennettii*. Propagation by seed or division. Floating leaves; planting depth 10–45 cm (4–18 in).

Orontium aquaticum (golden club) Araceae

A charming plant with large, dark, velvety green leaves with a silvery metallic sheen. The white, pencil-like flowers are tipped with yellow, looking like golden pokers. Start at a shallow depth in a large planting crate, and later lower into deeper water as it becomes established. Propagation by

Orontium aquaticum

seed or division. Height 30–45 cm
(1–1½ ft); planting depth 8–30 cm
(3–12 in).

Zantedeschia aethiopica (arum lily)
Araceae

A splendid pool plant, hardy only if
under 15 cm (6 in) of water. The leaves
are arrow-shaped and glossy on long,
smooth stems. A golden-yellow,
poker-like spadix is produced in the
centre of each pure white flower
(spathe). Introduce into shallow water
and gradually lower as it grows.
Height 90–120 cm (3–4 ft); planting
depth 15–30 cm (6–12 in).

FLOATING PLANTS

Azolla caroliniana (fairy moss)
Azollaceae

A tiny aquatic fern which form mats of
lacy fronds, only 0.75 cm (⅜ in). It is
pale green in summer, but as the
autumn approaches takes on rich tints
of red, crimson and brown. It is

advisable to overwinter a few stock
plants in a pan of loam covered with
about 2.5 cm (1 in) of water.

Eichhornia crassipes (water hyacinth)
Pontederiaceae

Perhaps the showiest of floating
plants, but as it is not frost hardy stock
plants should be overwintered indoors. The 5–15 cm (2–6 in) cordate

Opposite: *Pistia stratiotes* (see page 104)

Right: *Eichhornia crassipes*

leaves are smooth, dark green and shiny, with swollen stalks that look like small balloons; these are full of tiny air pockets, which enable it to float. In summer 15 cm (6 in) spikes bearing between ten and thirty beautiful, light purplish-blue flowers with yellow and blue markings are produced. Long – 60–90 cm (2–3 ft) – trails of purplish roots are ideal for spawning fish. Propagation is by means of stolons. It spreads at a prodigious rate and can become a serious problem to river navigation in many tropical countries.

Hydrocharis morsus-ranae (frogbit)
Hydrocharitaceae
An attractive little plant with small, round, fleshy, floating leaves and small white flowers. In autumn the plant drops resting buds that overwinter in the mud, rising to the surface in June to start off new plants. Propagation by stolons and overwintered buds.

LEMNA Lemnaceae

The duckweeds are a useful group of floating plants as they reduce the amount of light penetrating the water and so discourage growth of algae. They also provide a valuable source of fish food. Their prodigious rate of growth can easily be controlled by scooping out excess plants whenever necessary.

L. gibba (thick duckweed) Very small perennial floating plants with spongy fronds that multiply rapidly.

L. minor (common duckweed) A very vigorous species of floating plant, which although providing shade and food for fish can become a problem because of the rate at which it multiplies. The pale green fronds are flat, ovate, up to 0.5 cm ($\frac{1}{4}$ in) in diameter.

L. polyrrhiza (greater duckweed) Not quite as invasive a plant as *L. gibba* and *L. minor*. Green and red round fronds, their diameter up to 1 cm ($\frac{1}{2}$ in).

L. trisulca (ivy-leaved duckweed) This duckweed is worthy of inclusion because of its well restrained growth and attractive floating foliage, which is delicate, diamond-shaped and dark green in colour.

Pistia stratiotes (water lettuce)
Araceae
A tender floating plant which should be overwintered indoors. It is extremely attractive, producing rosettes of pale green, fan-shaped, velvety leaves about 15 cm (6 in) across. The roots are trailing and feathery, up to 15 cm (6 in) long. Propagation by offsets.

Stratiotes aloides (water soldier)
Hydrocharitaceae
An interesting plant 5–20 cm (2–8 in) long and 10–20 cm (4–8 in) wide with spiny rosettes of green, narrow, serrated leaves looking like the top of a pineapple. It floats just under the water until it blooms, when it rises to the surface, and produces small white flowers before sinking to the bottom of the pool for the winter. It is a good oxygenator. Propagation by sideshoots.

Trapa natans (water chestnut)
Trapaceae
This annual floating plant has triangular, serrated, dark green leaves with spongy leafstalks which enable them to float. The small white flowers, produced in late summer, are followed by large, edible black fruits, which sink to the bottom of the pond ready to produce fresh young plants the

following spring. Propagation by seed.

MOISTURE-LOVING PLANTS

Aruncus dioicus (goat's beard)
Rosaceae

Tall plants that look particularly effective in a shady area by the pool in June, with their minute, creamy-white flowers held in feathery panicles above the deep green, pinnate leaves. They may be grown in groups, or are bold enough to be grown as solitary specimens, particularly the male plants which have the more showy panicles. Propagation by division in October. Also known as *Aruncus sylvester*. Height 120–180 cm (4–6 ft).

Astilbe × arendsii
Saxifragaceae

A deservedly popular group, hybrid astilbes are easily grown in moist soils, forming neat, compact and wind-resistant plants of green pinnate foliage beneath feathery inflorescences in rich colours; the flowering period is June to August. Propagation is by division.

Recommended hybrids:

'Bonn' – bright rosy pink; height 60 cm (2 ft)

'Deutschland' – intense white; height 60 cm (2 ft)

'Fanal' – deep red spikes; height 75 cm (1½ ft)

'Rheinland' early flowering pink 60 cm (2 ft).

Bergenia cordifolia Saxifragaceae

Bergenias will grow in almost any soil, but they excel in the moist conditions of the poolside. The large, evergreen leaves are rounded with a heart-shaped base, often changing to tinges of red in the autumn. The pendulous heads of lilac-rose, bell-shaped flowers appear in spring. Propagate by division in spring or autumn. Height 30 cm (12 in).

Camassia leichtlinii Liliaceae

Hardy bulbs that can be left to flower from one year to the next, providing early splashes of star-shaped, white to blue flowers borne on terminal racemes above strap-shaped green leaves. Ideal for naturalizing and a good cut flower. Propagation by freshly gathered seed in summer or offsets from the bulbs, which are replanted immediately in September. Height 90 cm (3 ft).

DODECATHEON Primulaceae

These 'shooting stars' or 'American cowslips', as they are often known, have nodding, cyclamen-like flowers borne on leafless stems in early summer. They enjoy partial shade and should be left undisturbed to form clumps. The flowers vary in colour according to species, but are mainly in shades of pink, red and purple. Propagation by seed or division. The main species grown are:

D. *frigidum* – mauve-violet flowers;

D. *meadia* – rose-purple flowers with white bases and reddish yellow anthers;

D. *hendersonii* – purple flowers with yellow anthers.

Most of the species are 30–38 cm (12–15 in) high.

FILIPENDULA Rosaceae

Closely related to spiraeas, they are tolerant of both shade and sunny situations, and the light, feathery flowerheads are particularly attractive. Propagation is by division or seed. The following species are recommended.

Astilbe × arendsii
mixed cultivars
(see page 105)

Gunnera manicata

folded over quite easily until the danger of severe frosts is over. The inconspicuous green flowers are dense, cone-shaped panicles 90–120 cm (3–4 ft) long. Propagation by division, using the small young crowns that form around the old rootstock. Height 2–3 m (6–10 ft).

HEMEROCALLIS (day lily)
Liliaceae

There are many superb hybrids now available of these robust, free-flowering herbaceous perennials with their dense clumps of arching, grassy leaves. The flowers are trumpet shaped and available in a wide variety of colours from June to August, being replaced as each flower fades. Recommended cultivars include:

H. citrina Lemon yellow, slightly fragrant flowers. Height 90 cm (3 ft).
H. flava Scented, yellow lily-shaped flowers. Height 75 cm (2½ ft).
H. fulva var. **kwanso** Double orange flowers. Height 120 cm (4 ft).
H. fulva var. **rosea** Soft coppery-coloured flowers. Height 120 cm (4 ft).

F. palmata Flowers in July in shades of rose to pale pink. Height 90 cm (3 ft).
F. ulmaria (meadow sweet) Common as a native plant in Britain in streams and ditches, with creamy-white, fragrant flowers from June to August. Height 60–90 cm (2–3 ft).
F. ulmaria 'Aurea' Golden yellow leaves, most attractive for banks.
F. ulmaria 'Variegata' Leaves striped with yellow, this very attractive variegation has a tendency to revert to green.

Gunnera manicata Haloragaceae
One of the most impressive waterside plants, with its huge leaves often growing to 2 m (6 ft) or more. The young growth is susceptible to frost damage, and the leaves can be completely blackened overnight. The plant should be protected in winter and spring by covering the crowns with their own leaves. These can be

H. middendorffii Fragrant orange-yellow flowers. Height 30–60 cm (1–2 ft).

H. minor Scented clear yellow flowers. Height 30–45 cm (1–1½ ft).

H. thunbergii Fragrant sulphur-apricot flowers. Height 90 cm (3 ft).

HOSTA (plantain lily) Liliaceae

An excellent group of ornamental foliage plants with beautifully veined basal leaves that are the plant's main attraction. The flowers, produced from mid to late summer, are funnel-shaped, often fragrant, and borne on erect or ascending flowering stems. Hostas are at their best when planted in deep, rich, moist soil and left undisturbed, and are extremely effective when planted by water. Flower arrangers have increased the popularity of the genus, proving that they will tolerate a fairly wide range of soil types, though they never reach their full splendour unless in a very moist soil. Propagation is best achieved by carefully removing sections of clumps without disturbing the main plant.

H. crispula A species with broadly lanceolate leaves with a long point, wavy edged and margined with white. The flowers are 5 cm (2 in) long, lilac-purple, and produced in July and August. Height 60 cm (2 ft).

H. decorata Attractive dark green, ovate to elliptical leaves with wide white margins extending down the leaf stalks. The lilac-coloured flowers are produced in July. Height 60 cm (2 ft).

H. elata A very robust species forming mounds of pale green, matt, waxy edged foliage. The flowers are white to lilac-lavender, carried above the foliage in June and July. Also known as

Hosta crispula

H. fortunei var. *gigantea*. Height up to 90 cm (3 ft).

H. fortunei Beautiful long-stalked, grey-green, prominently veined ovate leaves about 13 cm (5 in) long. Lilac flowers in July. Height 60 cm (2 ft). Cultivars include:

'Albopicta' – an excellent plant with pale green young leaves broadly variegated with buff-yellow, deepening with age to a glaucous green; height 60 cm (2 ft).

Iris gracilipes likes moist but not waterlogged soil (see page 109)

'Aurea' – the young leaves are yellow, turning green with age; height 60–75 cm (2–2½ ft).

'Aureomarginata' – each leaf has a narrow gold margin; height 60–75 cm (2–2½ ft).

'Marginato-Alba' – striking sage-green leaves boldly edged with white, and lilac flowers from June to August; height 60–75 cm (2–2½ ft).

H. lancifolia Neat mounds are formed of narrow, lanceolate, glossy, dark green leaves which overlap each other, with lilac-coloured flowers borne on slender stems from July to September. Height 60 cm (2 ft).

H. longissima Plain green, linear to lanceolate leaves about 18 cm (7 in) long. Pale, rosy-purple flowers produced late in the season. Sold in the trade as H. japonica var. longifolia Height 45–60 cm (1½–2 ft).

H. plantaginea Cordate, bright green, glossy leaves. Fragrant white flowers 10–13 cm (4–5 in) long are produced during August and September. Height 60 cm (2 ft).

H. rectifolia The uniformly dark green leaves are lanceolate in shape. Elegant spikes bear beautiful violet-mauve flowers in August and September. Also called H. longipes. Height 90–120 cm (3–4 ft).

H. sieboldiana Attractive, heavily veined, grey-green leaves up to 38 cm (15 in) long, and pale lavender to white flowers produced in August. Also known as H. glauca. Height Height 60 cm (2 ft).

H. undulata This species has unusual and attractive mid-green leaves, which are variegated longitudinally with silver-white markings and have very wavy edges. The beautiful pale lilac flowers are produced in August. Height 60 cm (2 ft).

H. ventricosa A very reliable and free-flowering species, with wavy-edged, deep green, glossy leaves and violet-coloured flowers in August. Height 90 cm (3 ft).

H. ventricosa 'Variegata' This is outstanding with its rich green leaves with yellow striped margins. Violet-mauve flowers contrast beautifully, making this a highly desirable plant. Height 75 cm (2½ ft).

IRIS Iridaceae

The moist conditions of the water's edge provide a superb setting for many of the iris species, notably those referred to as the beardless iris. Most species have sword-like foliage in the shape of a fan, and an enormous variety of flower sizes and colours. Many of the species are at their best when massed on a bank at the water's edge, but they can also have great merit as individual groups on the very edge of a small formal or informal pool. Certain species will tolerate their roots under 5–10 cm (2–4 in) of water (see under Aquatic plants, page 80). Propagation by division.

I. bulleyana A good choice where space is limited, this small iris produces tuft-like grassy foliage with purple flowers and purple and cream blotches in the centre of the lower petals (falls). Height 45 cm (1½ ft).

I. chrysographes The flowers, which are produced in June, are deep violet with attractive gold markings, with some colour variations extending to an almost black form. The foliage is soft and grass-like, resembling the more common I. sibirica but smaller. Height 45 cm (1½ ft).

I. delavayi A fine species with attractive, grass-like foliage. The flowers, which are borne on stout stems, are an intense shade of violet with white markings. Height 90–120 cm (3–4 ft).

I. fulva (syn. *I. cuprea*) A swamp species with bright green leaves and coppery coloured flowers with purple veining. Also known as *I. cuprea*. Height 60 cm (2 ft).

I. gracilipes A dainty little species requiring moist acid soil. The slender leaves are dark green and glossy. Lavender-pink flowers appear on branched stems in April and May. Height 21 cm (9 in).

I. kaempferi see page 83.

I. laevigata see page 84.

I. pseudacorus see page 84.

I. versicolor see page 85.

LIGULARIA Compositae

A striking group of robust plants, ideal for sunny spots and moist ground. They will not thrive in dry conditions. Propagation by seed or division.

L. dentata **'Desdemona'** A handsome cultivar of a Chinese species with large, purplish, shiny leaves. Purple stems bear branching spikes of deep orange, daisy-like flowers from July to September. Also sold as *L. clivorum* 'Desdemona'. Height 120 cm (4 ft).

L. stenocephala **'The Rocket'** Formerly known as *Senecio przewalskii*. Quite one of the loveliest of the ligularias, with deep purplish-black stems bearing handsome jagged-edged leaves and tall, elegant spires of bright yellow flowers in July and August. Height 120–180 cm (4–6 ft).

LEUCOJUM (snowflake)
Amaryllidaceae

Some leucojums do exceptionally well in damp places, and once established they bloom profusely if left undisturbed. Propagation is by seed or by offsets when the groups appear too large.

L. aestivum (summer snowflake) Long, mid-green, strap-like leaves are followed by erect stems bearing white flowers with green-tipped petals resembling large snowdrops from April to June. An outstanding cultivar is 'Gravetye Giant', which is more vigorous than the species and will do well with its bulbs completely under water. Height 60 cm (2 ft).

L. vernum (spring snowflake) Another moisture lover, with narrower, strap-like leaves and white, green-tipped, fragrant flowers blooming in February and March. Height 15–23 cm (6–9 in). There is a more striking and vigorous variety *vagneri*, which grows up to 60 cm (2 ft).

LOBELIA Campanulaceae

The perennial species and hybrids of this genus provide some of the most effective and colourful plants for the waterside. The two species recommended below are not fully hardy and should be overwintered in frost-free greenhouses or frames before increasing stock by taking cuttings in spring. Their vivid displays of scarlet flowers are best appreciated if the plants are in full sun and preferably not too windswept a situation.

L. cardinalis see page 85.

*Phalaris
arundinaceae* 'Picta'
(see page 112)

Opposite:
Osmunda regalis
(see page 112)

Below: *Iris
pseudacorus* (see
page 84) suitable
for poolside as well
as pool margin

L.fulgens The vivid red flowers on tapering, erect stems are similar to *L.cardinalis*, but are enhanced by the deep red, almost purple foliage with toothed leaf margins. There are many excellent cultivars bred from this species, which, like their parent, are not hardy but extremely colourful. Height 90 cm (3 ft).

Lysimachia nummularia (creeping jenny) Primulaceae
This vigorous native of Britain is a good trailing ground cover plant, superb for covering banks with its prolific summer display of bright yellow, buttercup-like flowers. It shows a remarkable ability to adapt to a wide range of moisture regimes, from almost dry banks to submerged conditions. It must therefore be used with great care in case its vigour and desire for space suppress other small plants, particularly young self-sown primula seedlings. Propagation is by division or cuttings.
'**Aurea**' is similar to the species but has most attractive yellow leaves.

Matteuccia struthiopteris (ostrich plume fern) Onocleaceae
This beautiful fern has graceful, pale green sterile fronds arranged in a circle around a hard, scaly rootstock, making it look like a shuttlecock. Best grown in partial shade and moist soil. Propagation by offsets. Height 90 cm (3 ft).

MIMULUS (musk)
Scrophulariaceae

A very showy genus of moisture-loving annuals and perennials, forming spreading masses of light green foliage, and brilliant antirrhinum-shaped flowers. Unfortunately they may not survive severe winter weather, so must be protected or renewed most years. They have tolerance of a wide range of soil types and may meander happily into the water and grow on the submerged marginal shelves as well as being at home in drier conditions on a bank. Propagation by division, cuttings or seed.

M. × burnettii A hybrid between *M. cupreus* and *M. luteus*. The flowers are copper-yellow with yellow throats, blooming from May to August. The mid-green leaves are oblong-ovate. Height 25–30 cm (9–12 in).

M. cardinalis This species, which is more tolerant than most other *Mimulus* species, has hairy, ovate and sharply toothed leaves. The flowers are bright orange to scarlet with a yellow throat, produced from June to September. Protect from frost if possible. Height 45–60 cm (18–24 in).

M. lewisii Another species with hairy or downy leaves growing from thick, fleshy underground stems which are susceptible to severe winters and appreciate frost protection. The flowers are rose-pink, sometimes white, and are produced from July until the frosts arrive. Also known as *M. bartonianus*. Height 45 cm (18 in).

Onoclea sensibilis (sensitive fern) Onocleaceae
This attractive fern is ideal for a wet spot by the waterside, forming dense carpets of long-stemmed, pinky-coloured fronds in the spring which fade to a pale lime green. It turns brown at the first frost. Propagation by division or spores. Height 30–60 cm (1–2 ft).

Osmunda regalis (royal fern) Osmundaceae
Undoubtedly the most impressive of the hardy ferns, and at its best where the roots can easily reach water; over the years they form a mat, making a good edge to the pool. The handsome sterile fronds are pale green at first, turning to a rich russet brown in the autumn. The fertile fronds, which grow on separate stalks in the centre of the plant, are greenish brown. Propagation by division. Height 120–150 cm (4–5 ft).

Peltiphyllum peltatum (umbrella plant) Saxifragaceae
One of the early eye-catching flowers at the water's edge, the pink, rounded, saxifrage-like flowers appearing before the large, unusual, bronze green leaves, which, as the common name suggests, are umbrella-like and nearly 30 cm (1 ft) across. They are vigorous and need a deep soil, and have the bonus of spectacular autumn colours. Height 1.5 m (5 ft). There is a smaller cultivar, 'Nana', which is only 38 cm (15 in) high and strongly recommended for the smaller pool.

Phalaris arundinacea 'Picta' (gardener's garters) Graminae
This grass has bright, variegated young foliage, white tinged with pink; but must be planted with caution as it is invasive. The rather inconspicuous flowerheads are produced in June and July. It is an often underrated plant which is tough and bright, being particularly useful for difficult areas where the choicer plants may not succeed. Propagation by division. Height 75–90 cm (2½–3 ft).

Polygonum campanulatum Polygonaceae
Many of the polygonums, or knot-weeds, are very vigorous and invasive, but as they are relatively tolerant of shade they can be used to fill difficult gaps. This species, while being vigorous and fast spreading, has shallow roots and is therefore more controllable. The pink flowers are at their best from mid summer to autumn, with ovate leaves which are distinctly veined, dark green above and silvery beneath. Propagation by division. Height 60–120 cm (2–4 ft).

PRIMULA Primulaceae

A genus which provides some of the most showy as well as some of the choicest plants for the bog garden. Most primulas require rich, cool, retentive soil which must never be allowed to dry out at any stage of growth. Many of the bog primulas belong to the Candelabra, so called because the flowers are arranged in whorls around the upper part of the stem. Propagation is by division in spring or by seed, which in many cases must be sown fresh. Within the genus there are many excellent species, and the following list represents many of the best for waterside conditions.

P. aurantiaca The reddish-orange flowers are borne on reddish stems in June and July. The mid-green, narrowly obovate leaves have red veins. Height 20–30 cm (9–12 in).

P. beesiana Whorls of fragrant, velvety, brilliant purple-carmine flowers in June to July. The rough-textured leaves are light green and oblong-obovate in shape. Height 60 cm (2 ft).

P. bulleyana A very beautiful species with whorls of orange-yellow flowers in bloom from June to July. The thin leaves are dark green and oblong-obovate. Various colour forms are available. Height 60–90 cm (2–3 ft).

P. burmanica A handsome species bearing rigid stems with whorls of deep crimson-purple flowers from June to July. Mid-green, oblanceolate leaves. Height 60–90 cm (2–3 ft).

P. denticulata (drumstick primrose) One of the earliest flowering moisture-loving primulas, with large umbels of lavender flowers that appear before the leaves really develop. The broad leaves are pale green and farinose, forming rosettes. The colour forms can vary from white and pale lilac to deep purple, or rose to deep carmine. Propagation can be carried out by root cuttings. Height 30–60 cm (1–2 ft).

P. florindae (giant cowslip) This species produces strong stems bearing immense umbels of bell-shaped, sulphur-yellow, fragrant, nodding flowers in June and July. The leaves, which are toothed and mid-green in colour, grow to a length of 45 cm (18 in). Height 90–120 cm (3–4 ft).

P. helodoxa The stout stems produce many whorls of brilliant yellow flowers surrounded by light green leaves which remain throughout the winter. Height 60–90 cm (2–3 ft).

P. japonica (Japanese primrose) Perhaps the showiest and most popular of bog primulas, producing tall stems with whorl upon whorl of large, crimson-coloured flowers, in bloom from May to July. The pale green, oblong-obovate leaves grow in rosettes. To compensate for being somewhat short lived, the plants seed themselves freely, producing many colour forms of white, pink and crimson flowers, some with contrasting centres. Two cultivars worthy of note are 'Postford White', which has white flowers from May to July with a yellow eye, and 'Miller's Crimson', with crimson-red flowers in June. Height 60–75 cm (2–2½ ft).

P. pulverulenta An attractive species bearing several whorls of crimson flowers of fairy-like daintiness on white, farinose stems. The leaves are obovate or oblanceolate and pale green in colour. The Bartley strain is a varietal group producing a delightful range of pastel shades from buff through apricot to pink. Two of its hybrids worthy of note are 'Red

Schizostylis coccinea

Hugh' with brick red flowers, and 'Inverewe', with vivid scarlet-orange flowers, which is a sterile hybrid and can be propagated only by division. Height 60–90 cm (2–3 ft).

P. rosea An extremely delightful and choice dwarf species, carrying a profusion of intense rose-pink flowers which are borne in heads similar to those of the polyanthus. The close tufts of narrow, pale green, toothed leaves are flushed red and age to soft green. 'Delight' is even more lovely, with larger and brighter pink flowers. Height 15 cm (6 in).

P. sikkimensis (Himalayan cowslip) A beautiful primula with smooth stems carrying clustered heads of drooping, delicately perfumed, soft yellow flowers in June and July. The long, narrow leaves are pale green, finely toothed, and grow in rosettes. Height 45–60 cm ($1\frac{1}{2}$–2 ft).

P. vialii A very distinctive plant with poker-like spikes 8–13 cm (3–5 in) long of brilliant purple and red flowers borne on erect stalks. The slightly farinose, pale green leaves grow in tufts. Propagation by division or seed. Height 23–30 cm (9–12 in).

Rheum palmatum (ornamental rhubarb) Polygonaceae

This handsome species is best treated as a specimen plant, requiring a good deal of space in order to appreciate the fine, deeply cut leaves which take time to grow to their full potential. The spiraea-like flowers are produced in June on panicles 60–90 cm (2–3 ft) long. Propagation is by division of the old crowns in winter, ensuring that the offspring have a dormant bud present. There are some good cultivars, such as 'Atrosanguineum', which has deeply dissected leaves, and 'Rubrum', with deeply cut red leaves; both have crimson flowers and fruits. Height 1.5–2.5 m (5–8 ft).

Rodgersia pinnata Saxifragaceae

This plant, grown more for its beautiful foliage than its flowers, loves moist soils, but needs shelter from wind, and partial shade. It has thick, rhizomatous roots which take some time to become established. The flowerheads are panicles of starry flowers, ranging from white to pink and red. The luxuriously bronzed foliage is pinnately divided and a dark olive-green colour. Propagation is by division in spring or by seed. Height 90–120 cm (3–4 ft).

Rodgersia pinnata

Schizostylis coccinea (Kaffir lily)
Iridaceae
An attractive plant with fine sword-shaped leaves of mid green and flowers not unlike small gladioli. It revels in wet conditions and is very late flowering, from October onwards, bearing red or pink flowers. Propagation by division. Height 30–60 cm (1–2 ft). Cultivars of note include:
'Mrs Hegarty' – pale pink
'November Cheer' – rosy-red
'Viscountess Byng' – pale rose-pink.

***Spartina pectinata* 'Aureo-'Marginata'** (cord grass) Graminae
A cultivar of *S. pectinata*, which has green, ribbon-like leaves striped with yellow and drooping at the tips. Green flowers appear in the autumn. Propagation by division. Height 120 cm (4 ft).

Trollius (globe flower)
Ranunculaceae
Trollius resemble very large, globular buttercup flowers, which, although they flower in any reasonable soil, are only at their best right on the water's edge where the roots can have ample water. The flowers are held on stout stems well above the green foliage and flower in May and June. Propagation is by seed or by division. Most of the recommended cultivars are hybrids with the European *T. europaeus*. There is also a small species. *T. pumilis*, from China which is only half the height of *T. europaeus*, and suitable even for rock gardens. Height 60 cm (2 ft).

Lobelia cardinalis (see page 85) another aquatic plant suitable for poolside or bog garden

HARDY WATERLILIES FOR THE GARDEN POOL

	Red flowers
Smaller waterlilies adaptable to water **15–23 cm (6–9 in) deep**	N. × laydekeri 'Fulgens' N. × laydekeri 'Purpurata' N. pygmaea 'Rubra' 'Ellisiana' 'Froebeli'
Medium waterlilies adaptable to water **23–45 cm (9–18 in) deep**	'Gloriosa' 'James Brydon' 'Lucida'
Medium waterlilies adaptable to water **23–60 cm (9–24 in) deep**	'Atropurpurea' 'Conqueror' 'Escarboucle' 'Newton' 'René Gérard' 'William Falconer'
Waterlilies adaptable to water **30–75 cm (12–30 in) deep**	
Vigorous waterlilies adaptable to water **38–90 cm (15–36 in) deep**	'Attraction' 'Charles de Meurville'

(See also *Nymphaea* on pages 88–96)

Pink flowers	White flowers	Shades of yellow, copper, orange flowers
N. × laydekeri 'Liliacea'	N. candida N. odorata var. minor N. pygmaea 'Alba' 'Hermine'	'Aurora' 'Helvola' 'Paul Hariot'
'Helen Fowler' 'Lustrous' 'Mary Patricia' 'Odalisque' 'Pink Opal' 'Rose Arey' 'Somptuosa'	'Albatross' 'Loose'	'Comanche' 'Graziella' 'Indiana' 'Sulphurea Grandiflora'
N. odorata var. rosea 'Masaniello' 'Mme. Wilfron Gonnêre' 'Pink Sensation'	'Gonnêre' 'Hal Miller' N. odorata var. alba	'Moorei' 'Sunrise'

N. × marliacea 'Carnea'
N. × marliacea 'Rosea'
'Amabilis'
	N. × marliacea
	   'Albida'
	'Gloire de Temple-
	   sur-Lot'
	'Virginalis'
		N. × marliacea
		   'Chromatella'

N. tuberosa var. rosea 'Colossea' 'Mrs Richmond'	N. alba N. tuberosa 'Richardsonii' 'Gladstoniana'	'Colonel A.J. Welch'

Glossary

cordate Heart-shaped at base of leaf.

crown Upper part of a fleshy or woody rootstock from which shoots arise.

dissected leaf Divided into numerous narrow lobes.

falls Used to describe iris flowers; the three, usually larger, outer perianth segments ('petals') which have a reflexed blade, hence 'falling' outwards.

farinose Covered with a powdery or flour-like bloom; a particular characteristic of some primulas.

filamentous Threadlike.

flocculate Encouraging a number of small particles to join together to form larger ones. This is a way of improving clay soils by coarsening the texture and thus their drainage and workability.

free-floating plant Aquatic plants whose roots do not need anchorage in soil.

inflorescence The arrangement of flowers on the pedicel or flower stalk.

lanceolate Tapered towards each end, with the broadest point below the middle.

marginal Aquatic plants whose roots like to grow in shallow water around the pool edge.

oblanceolate Tapered towards each end, with the broadest point above the middle.

obovate With the broadest point above the middle.

ovate With the broadest point below the middle.

panicle A branched raceme.

pedicel A stalk of an individual flower.

perianth The outer, usually showy part of a flower, in monocotyledons such as irises it normally consists of six segments, often in two whorls (circles).

petiole A leaf stalk.

pinnate Leaflets arranged on either side of a central stalk.

protozoan Belonging to the Protozoa, a phyllum of animals consisting of a single cell.

raceme A type of flower arrangement, as in hostas and bluebells, where there is an elongated central axis with flowers carried separately along its length, each on its own pedicel or stalk.

reflexed The tips of petals or perianth segments that bend back, as in a dodecatheon flower.

rhizome A storage organ that is really a modified stem and capable of producing shoots and roots. It normally progresses horizontally and may be below ground or level with the surface (as in many irises).

Opposite:
Lysichitum americanum (see page 85)

rosette A cluster of leaves densely packed together in a wheel-like form, often flat on the ground but sometimes partially upright.

runner A rooting stem or stolon produced at soil level and forming a new plant which eventually becomes detached from the parent.

sepal The outer part of a flower bud that opens to reveal the petals and stamens.

serrated Leaves with a toothed or saw-edged margin.

spadix The thick, fleshy, pencil-like organ of an arum 'flower' which carries many very small male and female flowers near the base.

spathe A modified, usually papery leaf which encloses the whole flower cluster in the bud stage; in callas, lysichitums and other arums it is the most conspicuous part of the 'flower'.

spike A raceme (see page 119) in which the individual flowers have no stalks; it is thus usually a very dense inflorescence.

stamen The male portion of the flower, which produces pollen and consists of the filament (stalk) and anther (pollen-bearing part).

standard In iris flowers, the three inner perianth segments ('petals') which stand erect.

stellate Star-shaped.

stolon A creeping stem produced at soil level (see runner).

strap-like A leaf or petal that is parallel-sided like a belt or strap, rather wider than linear.

tuber A swollen underground organ that is solid, unlike a bulb which is scaly.

umbel A type of inflorescence in which the flowers all arise from the same point at the apex of a stem, like the spokes of an umbrella, as in the case of butomus, the flowering rush.

whorl Leaves or flowers that arise all from the same point on a stem in a circle around it, as in the case of candelabra primulas.

Bibliography

Heritage, W. *Ponds and Water Gardens*. Blandford Press, 1981.

Kaye, R. *Modern Water Gardening*. Faber and Faber, 1973.

Muhlberg, H. *The Complete Guide to Water Plants*. E. P. Publishing Ltd, 1982.

Perry, Frances *The Water Garden*. Ward Lock, 1981.

Stanley, R. *Stapeley Book of Water Gardening*. David and Charles, 1985.

Stodola, J. *Encyclopedia of Water Plants*. T. F. H. Publications Ltd, 1967.

Swindells, P. *Waterlilies*. Croom Helm, 1983.

Thomas, G. S. *Perennial Garden Plants or the Modern Florilegium*. Dent, 1982, rev. ed.

Curtis's *Botanical Magazine* (now *The Kew Magazine*). This publication still maintains its long tradition of fine colour printing and articles on plants, plant collecting and conservation. Since it was established in 1787 nearly 10,500 colour plates have appeared by many of the best British botanical artists.

Acknowledgements

Line artwork by David Bryant

Photographs

Biophotos/Heather Angel, pages 22, 31, 67, 70, 99; Pat Brindley, pages 58, 62, 63, 66, 82 (top and bottom), 86 (top and bottom), 87, 90 (bottom), 91, 94 (top), 95, 98, 102 (top and bottom), 103, 106, 107 (left, top right and bottom right), 110 (top and bottom), 111, 114 (top and bottom); Crown copyright © reproduced with the permission of the Controller, Her Majesty's Stationery Office, and the Director, Royal Botanic Gradens, Kew, pages 6, 10; Derbyshire Countryside/ADLIB Foto Agency, page 14; Jerry Harpur, page 118; S. & O. Mathews, page 39: The Photo Source/Colour Library International, pages 78–9; Photos Horticultural, pages 50, 54, 115; Peter Robinson, pages 18, 26, 34, 43, 46 (top, centre and bottom), 47 (top, centre and bottom); John Simmons, pages 19, 38; The Harry Smith Horticultural Photographic Collection, pages 27, 30, 35, 42, 71, 74, 75 (top and bottom), 83, 90 (top), 94 (bottom).

Taxonomy checked by Susyn Andrews, who works as a botanist at the Royal Botanic Gardens, Kew, and is also a member of the *Kew Magazine* Editorial Committee. She studied amenity horticulture at the National Botanic Gardens, Glasnevin, Co. Dublin, Republic of Ireland.

Index